HOW

PSYCHOMETRIC

4th ed.

TESTS

'Every man is like every other man, like some other men, like no other man.'

Clyde Kluckhohn, Anthropologist

HOW TO MASTER

PSYCHOMETRIC TESTS

Expert advice on test preparation with
practice questions from leading
test providers

4th edition

MARK PARKINSON

**KOGAN
PAGE**

London and Philadelphia

Whilst the author has made every effort to ensure that the content of this book is accurate, please note that occasional errors can occur in books of this kind. If you suspect that an error has been made in any of the tests included in this book, please inform the publisher at the address printed below so that it can be corrected at the next reprint.

Publisher's note
Every possible effort has been made to ensure that the information contained in this book is accurate at the time of going to press, and the publishers and author cannot accept responsibility for any errors or omissions, however caused. No responsibility for loss or damage occasioned to any person acting, or refraining from action, as a result of the material in this publication can be accepted by the editor, the publisher or the author.

First published in 1997
Second edition 2000
Third edition 2004
Reprinted 2005, 2006, 2007
Fourth edition 2008

120 Pentonville Road
London N1 9JN
United Kingdom
www.koganpage.com

525 South 4th Street, #241
Philadelphia PA 19147
USA

© Mark Parkinson 1997, 2000, 2004, 2008

ISBN 978 0 7494 5165 3

British Library Cataloguing-in-Publication Data

A CIP record for this book is available from the British Library.

Library of Congress Cataloging-in-Publication Data

Parkinson, Mark.
 How to master psychometric tests : expert advice on test preparation with practice questions from leading test providers / Mark Parkinson. -- 4th ed. p.cm.
 ISBN 978-0-7494-5165-3
 1. Employment tests. 2. Psychological tests. 3. Psychological tests--Problems, exercise, etc. 4. Psychometrics. 5. Employee selection. I. Title
 HF5549.5.E5P37 2008
 153.9'465--dc22
                                2008001466

Typeset by Jean Cussons Typesetting, Diss, Norfolk
Printed and bound in India by Replika Press Pvt Ltd

Contents

To the reader

Psychometric tests of ability and personality are used by many organizations throughout the world for selecting people for jobs. They are also used within companies to help with development and promotion.

This book is about preparing you for the main types of tests and increasing your chances of getting to the next stage, the job interview. This is a vital step in the selection process when you consider that 50 per cent or more people fail the tests they take.

All of the tests described in this book are commonly used for recruitment purposes. My job has been to explain what they measure, what they look like, who they are used to assess and how to approach the questions. The focus is on developing an effective test-making strategy or a personal approach that you can apply to any new test you might encounter.

I also concentrate on the psychological preparation for tests, and how to put yourself in a positive and winning frame of mind. This is just as important to test performance as understanding how the actual questions work.

This is the fourth edition of this book. It has been completely revised and now includes practice material from three leading UK test publishers. There is also an example of the type of test used to help select students for popular degree courses. In addition there is an interesting section on the 'dark side' of personality and a specially written Leadership Style Questionnaire.

Finally, it includes a unique list of the top 50 practice test websites, giving access to thousands of extra practice questions.

Introduction

If you were a personnel manager how would you select new staff?

Probably you would place a job advert and ask people to send a curriculum vitae (CV), or to complete an application form. Then you might look at the forms and invite, depending on how many people applied, between 6 and 12 people to come for an interview. After the interviews, or maybe at the same time, you would follow up references on the best candidates. If this is all you would do, you would be ignoring a technique that has become an essential part of the modern selection process – the psychometric test.

Application forms or CVs are an exercise in seeing how well an applicant, or frequently an agency, can fill in a form or design a work history. Interviews are an example of how prepared a candidate is for a number of standard questions, and of appearing to be interested and motivated for a short period of time. The reference, *at worst*, damns with faint praise, even if the subject has previously been an entirely unsatisfactory employee. In contrast, psychometric tests can identify objectively where the abilities lie, and what sort of personality you have. So as long as the appropriate tests are used, they can provide a fair and accurate way of helping to pick the best person for the job.

Tests are also desirable because not everyone is a good interview candidate, but many may still be ideal candidates for the job; and application forms are sometimes so badly designed that it is difficult to present yourself in a positive light. Conversely, skilled CV authors or interviewees may be quite hopeless when they actually secure a position. What this means is that in most circumstances it is to the applicant's *and* employer's advantage that tests are used.

To cut a long story short, what employers want to know is whether you can do a particular job and if you will fit into an existing workplace. This has more to do with your potential abilities and personality than the number of examination passes you have, or whether you liked going to school or college. Since tests are probably the most efficient way of assessing these factors, it should come as no surprise to discover that most medium- to large-sized organizations now use this method of selection.

So, in reality, when you apply for a job, whether this is through a job agency, cold canvassing, an advert in a newspaper or via details held on a website (recruitment information on the world wide web), the next step for the 'successful' candidate is frequently a series of psychometric tests.

Which tests are used?

In the UK, USA and many European countries the most popular tests are those of general intelligence, verbal and numerical ability, and personality. General intelligence tests are concerned with how well you can solve problems from first principles; verbal and numerical tests with aspects of verbal and numerical comprehension, and problem solving; and personality questionnaires with attributes like how outgoing you are, your degree of anxiety or emotionality, mental toughness and personal organization.

In the UK, if you are invited to attend a test session you will find yourself taking the sort of tests just described. This will be true of virtually all the major retail, manufacturing and service companies, as well as government and some educational and non-profit making organizations. Indeed, over 70 per cent of the *Times Top 1000* companies use tests of this nature. The picture is similar if you apply for jobs in many European Union countries, although some supplement testing with other techniques. For example, in France about 60 per cent of the top companies use tests, but 80 per cent also use graphology or handwriting analysis! The same is true in Germany, where, while around 60 per cent of firms use 'assessment centres', which include tests, interviews and other exercises, great weight is still placed on application forms and reference checks.

Make no mistake, tests are here to stay, so it makes sense to prepare yourself thoroughly for what has become a routine part of the job application process.

About this book

The first chapter of this book looks at the concept of psychometric testing. It explores the different types of tests, and the ways in which they measure both maximum and typical performance. The idea of 'intelligence' is introduced, as well as the differences between tests that measure knowledge (attainment) and potential (aptitude). An explanation of what makes a 'good' test is given, and also how we know that tests actually work. The chapter concludes with details on what employers do with test results, and the different ways in which they can be used to select candidates for jobs.

The next chapter explains the testing process and takes you through a typical selection scenario. This includes the basics of test preparation, and includes what you need to consider before a test session. The problems of test-taking anxiety ('examination nerves') are explained, and a number of methods of reducing anxiety are provided. Additional advice is given on preparing physically and emotionally for tests; and what to do if you have eyesight, hearing or other problems.

Chapter 3 covers, in separate sections, tests of abstract (logical), verbal, numerical, perceptual (diagrammatic), spatial and mechanical ability. The nature and purpose of each type of test is explained, and a number of examples are provided. An explanation of how to approach and to solve each example question is given. Each section also includes information on the sort of candidates who would face each test, eg if you are a graduate the sort of tests you would be asked to complete. Some practical hints are included for each type of test. The chapter concludes with 10 additional ways to improve test performance.

Chapter 4 contains an extensive collection of practice material from Saville & Holdsworth Ltd (SHL®). SHL is the leading UK test publisher and supplies assessment materials to most of the FTSE Top 100 companies as well as many smaller organizations. The practice tests are just like their full-length cousins and are arranged in three levels of difficulty. Readers will be comforted to know that the answers are provided at the end of the book!

Chapter 5 includes additional practice questions from one of the most innovative publishers in the marketplace, Team Focus Ltd. The example questions provided are typical of those that are now used for paper-and-pencil and internet based testing. In the second part of this chapter there is a discussion of a relatively new development in testing in the UK, the university admissions test. To illustrate what these tests are like, a section of a genuine practice test, the Thinking Skills Assessment (TSA), is included. This has been supplied by Cambridge Assessment, which is the business name of the University of Cambridge Local Examinations Syndicate (UCLES). Answers to all the practice questions are provided at the end of the book.

Chapter 6 concentrates on the ideas behind personality assessment, and describes the two main models that underpin personality questionnaires. These are the 'type' approach, which emphasises preferences for different sorts of behaviour; and the 'trait' school, which concentrates on direction and 'quantity' of personality. Extensive details on the format of 'self-report' questionnaires are included, as well as information on how different questionnaires are used. A list of hints for improving performance is provided, such as how to decide what an employer is looking for, and how to assume the correct test-taking attitude. Finally, other self-report questionnaires, such as those measuring values, motivation, integrity and interests, are explained.

Chapter 7 provides a list of the top 50 practice test websites. These sites provide an important resource for anyone preparing for a test session, be this either for a job, or when applying for popular university courses.

The appendix contains useful information on 'competencies', or the work attributes that tests are designed to measure; plus an example of the sort of exercise used by employers simultaneously to assess a group of job applicants.

In conclusion, this book is about helping you to understand the sort of psychometric tests that you may be asked to complete. It also includes details on how to prepare for tests and what to do if you are nervous about the testing process. The main sections deal with the most popular ability tests and personality questionnaires, and provide up-to-date information on:

- what different types of test measure;
- when they are used in selection;
- what the questions look like;
- how to answer typical questions;
- successful strategies and approaches.

The idea is to give you a set of practical tools, which will boost your chances of achieving test and career success. In this way *How to Master Psychometric Tests* will appeal to all those seeking employment with organizations that use tests. It will also be valuable to those who are tested while working within an organization for development or promotional purposes; and to employers, personnel and human resource professionals unfamiliar with psychometric tests, but who want to know more about what they are and how they can be used.

Note: Masculine pronouns are used in this book to avoid awkward grammatical constructions. In most cases, feminine pronouns can be used interchangeably.

1

What are psychometric tests?

A psychometric test is a standard way of measuring an aspect of mental performance. Practically this means that tests assess things like verbal ability, such as how good you are at understanding the meaning of words, or comprehending the information in a written passage. They are also used to explore personal attributes like personality or temperament, careers or employment interests, values, attitudes and motivation.

The fact that tests are *standard* methods of assessment is extremely important, and is what makes them different from the 'Personality' and 'Check your own Intelligence' quizzes found in magazines. Psychometric tests are different because everyone is presented with the same questions and instructions for completing them. Crucially, tests are also administered under carefully controlled and timed conditions by a trained individual, who additionally follows precise instructions for scoring and interpreting the results. In this way there is no room for subjectivity, and everyone is treated in exactly the same way. Furthermore, the results a person achieves are compared with a representative sample of people (the normative group) who have completed the test before. This allows a psychologist or personnel professional to decide accurately how well a person has done compared to everyone else. Is the person above or below average? How much is the person above or below?

These features of psychometric tests are also what distinguish them from most forms of examinations. It's true that examinations are timed and that everyone attempts the same paper, but there are usually a variety of questions to choose from. In an essay-based exam it is also the case that there are a number of possible answers to the questions. Clearly some answers will be better than others, and so there are a range of marks on offer. The marking system obviously has to reflect these differences, and so cannot but fail to reflect some of the personal preferences of the examiner. All of this makes most examinations rather less objective than a well-constructed psychometric test.

Personality questionnaires differ in a number of ways from ability tests simply because there are no 'right' or 'wrong' answers. After all there is no such thing as a 'good' or 'bad' personality, just a variety of personal characteristics, which may be more or less useful depending on what you are trying to do. However, despite the nature of what is being measured, personality questionnaires still contain questions that everyone must answer; and are administered, scored and interpreted in a standard way.

Different types of tests

For most purposes psychologists distinguish between two broad types of tests. The first type is concerned with measuring maximum performance, or how well you can do something. This means that they measure what you know, or what your potential might be, when you are trying to do as well as you can.

The second type of test measures typical performance. In consequence these are concerned with finding out what you are like in normal, day-to-day situations. For instance, are you outgoing and sociable, or do you prefer your own company?

Personality questionnaires are an example of this second sort of test, and are particularly useful in those situations where job performance is dependent on how you present yourself to other people, eg all forms of selling activity.

Returning to tests of maximum performance, we find that practically all the ability tests you will be asked to complete as part of a selection process fall into this category. To be even more precise they can also be classified as follows:

- general intelligence tests;
- attainment tests; and
- aptitude tests.

General intelligence tests

Some tests are formulated so that they measure your overall ability to succeed in a particular activity. These are known as general intelligence tests and are designed to produce a single indication of your ability. This is similar to the concept of the intelligence quotient or IQ. Although in the case of IQ tests the results are expressed in terms of the ratio of your mental age (as measured by a test) to your chronological age, with the resultant multiplied by 100. Thus, if your mental and chronological age are the same you end up with the average IQ of 100. All tests of this sort operate on the principle that your 'general intelligence' affects all of your individual abilities. So, for example, it's your overall intelligence that makes you good or bad at things like verbal or numerical problem solving.

Attainment tests

Attainment tests measure your ability to use the knowledge or skills you already possess. So, if you like, they are designed to assess what you know at the time of the test. For example, can you understand a simple electrical circuit, or do you know the name of the second-highest mountain in the world? However, you could ask yourself whether this really is 'typical' performance in the sense of the ability you will bring to a job. Also, most attainment tests demand a knowledge of things that may not generalize to every aspect of a job.

Some attainment tests are described as mastery tests. These are based on specific tasks, which directly relate to a particular work activity. They are also characterized by the fact that there are only two outcomes; you either 'pass' or 'fail'. The driving test is an example, because you either pass and are permitted to drive a car on the road, or you fail and have to take the test again. Most professional examinations are also mastery tests. This is a sensible thing if you imagine the chaos that would ensue if there were different pass grades for something like medical or dental examinations. Would you go to a particular doctor or dentist if you knew he had only just managed to pass his exams?

Another sort of attainment test it's useful to know about is the work sample test. These are tests based on the things you actually do in a particular job. For instance, giving someone a typing test, which involves measuring their ability to type a dictated letter accurately, is a work sample test. Another example is the 'in-tray' or 'in-basket' exercise used in executive assessment centres. This involves presenting a candidate with a number of letters, faxes, e-mails, reports, computer printouts, invoices and other pieces of information, and asking for them to be put in order of priority and actioned accordingly. This is a highly stressful test, maybe, but one that does simulate the work required of many managers.

The most advanced form of work sample test is the aircraft simulator. This allows skills to be assessed, and training to take place, in a safe and cost-effective manner. In fact modern simulators are so realistic that most, if not all, basic training can take place without the pilot ever leaving the hangar. Indeed, legend has it that at least one airline has used pilots who have done all their advanced training on the ground!

Aptitude tests

Aptitude tests measure your 'natural' ability to do things. Unlike attainment tests they do not require specialist knowledge or skills. Obviously some understanding is involved, if only to comprehend the instructions, but as far as possible the results are designed to reflect your potential to achieve in the future. This makes the aptitude tests a fairer assessment for anyone who lacks traditional school qualifications; or who just hasn't had the opportunity to acquire specific skills.

Aptitude tests are frequently used for careers counselling, and also form a useful tool for any employer who wishes to identify potential. Like work-related measures many aptitude tests are constructed so that they indicate whether a person is suitable for a particular job, eg computer programming. However, in contrast to the work sample approach, they do not assume that you have a range of existing skills. The argument is that if you have the potential you can be taught to write programs, calculate exchange rates, compose a technical report, or whatever. Naturally there is also a counter-argument, which suggests that aptitude tests do not relate to real job tasks and do not measure experience. This is an interesting point and one that highlights the essential difference between the attainment and aptitude approaches.

You might have noticed in the descriptions of attainment and aptitude tests that they seem to relate to specific abilities. That's because, in contrast to the general intelligence approach, they rely on the idea of different types of intelligence. In many ways this is a far more useful approach because it recognizes the fact that we all have different combinations of abilities. It also recognizes that one factor, general intelligence, does not dictate everything we can do.

As you might expect, some psychologists believe in the general intelligence approach, and others in the existence of many separate, specific abilities. However, in the real world of work it is usually your specific abilities, whether they be attainment or aptitude based, which are measured in a test session.

What is a 'good' test?

Whatever sort of test is used to assess someone for a job, it must fulfil a number of important requirements. From the employer's point of view it should obviously be cost-effective, relevant to the position in question, and fair on the people applying. Even more importantly, the test, or tests, must actually work. This depends on the standard administration and objective scoring mentioned earlier, but, even more crucially, on any tests being reliable and valid.

Reliability is all about getting consistent results over time. For example, if I tested you today, and then again in four weeks' time, I would expect to get more or less the same results. I wouldn't expect your abilities to have changed, unless you had learnt something in the interim; or, indeed, for something like your personality to have altered significantly. However, being reliable is not enough because it is possible to achieve consistent results and still not be measuring anything meaningful. A good example is the 'buttercup test' we used as children.

If you hold a buttercup under your chin on a sunny day it will cast a yellow shadow. This is supposed to indicate a liking for butter. However, as you will no doubt appreciate, if it's sunny you will always get a yellow spot on your chin. It's a very reliable test, but unfortunately there is no real link between yellow shadows and butter appreciation.

Clearly it's not enough for a test to be reliable, it must be valid as well. Indeed validity, or the extent to which a test measures what the designer says it's measuring, is the most fundamental attribute of any measure. However, validity is rather a complicated thing to establish, and to confuse things further there are a number of different types.

For example, face validity refers to the extent to which a test measures what it looks as if it's measuring. If a test is designed to assess numerical ability you would expect it to contain mathematical problems. You would not expect it to have a lot of highly verbal items, or ask you about how you prefer to socialize with other people.

While face validity is important it does not guarantee that a test works (think about the magazine 'tests' mentioned at the beginning of this chapter); so it's important to establish what is known as criterion-related validity. This is also sometimes called external validity and is the degree to which a test correlates with another measure of the same thing. For instance, you might expect a numerical test to correlate with mathematical ability, as measured by a formal examination. Yet, important as this might be, the ultimate sort of external validity is predictive validity. This sort of validity is when we can demonstrate that a test predicts a future measure of performance. Put simply, if I give you a particular test, can I say that if you achieve a certain score there is an increased chance of you being a more productive employee?

To summarize what we have learnt in this chapter so far, a 'good' test should be as follows.

- **Objective.** Each person who takes it should be treated in exactly the same way. The scoring and interpretation of the results should be conducted according to the directions laid down by the test designer.
- **Standardized.** The score a person gets on the test should be compared against a representative group of people who have taken the test in the past (the normative group). Any decisions should then only be made in comparison with this standard group.
- **Reliable.** The test must consistently measure the same thing, with no marked differences over time. The exception, of course, is where we use an attainment test and wish to measure what you have learnt over a period of time.
- **Predictive.** The test must be a valid measure of what it's supposed to measure. It is also important to establish that it's an accurate predictor of how someone will perform in the future.
- **Unbiased.** The test should only measure an aspect of maximum or typical performance. It should not discriminate in terms of race, culture, gender or any similar factor.

Naturally there may be differences between different groups, but these must only be due to actual differences in ability or personality, and not just a product of the way a test is worded or constructed.

Considering these requirements, it should now be obvious that writing a test is a complex process, and perhaps not the 'armchair' exercise many people imagine it to be. Then again, the fact that 'good' tests conform to all these requirements should be a comfort to the potential test taker. After all, tests are used to assess people for one of life's most taxing environments – the workplace.

How are test results used?

There are a number of ways in which tests results can be used to assess people. However, the prime objective of all these methods is to identify at an early stage those job applicants who are unlikely to fill the requirements of the position on offer. They do this by providing a scientific benchmark against which all applicants can be assessed. In this way ability test results can be used to supply information on current knowledge or performance; and personality questionnaires the sort of insights that are difficult to achieve in a 45- or 60-minute interview.

A warning should be sounded at this point because, while what has just been said is correct, the usefulness of any testing process depends on knowing exactly what you are looking for in the first place. This depends on a comprehensive analysis of the job, or jobs, in question. It's only after the personnel professional or psychologist has established a specification for a job that meaningful comparisons can be made. Thus in the normal course of events information is gathered on the following.

- **Knowledge.** Is a specialist sort of knowledge required? For example, do you need an in-depth understanding of legal terms and procedures?
- **Skills.** Are particular skills crucial to good performance? For example, are certain computer or IT (information technology) skills essential?
- **Abilities.** Are particular underlying abilities considered necessary? For example, do you need an aptitude for verbal or numerical problem solving?
- **Experience.** Is a certain type or range of experience valuable? For example, is experience of doing business in different countries required?

Sometimes these different sorts of job requirements are combined into what are called competencies. These are 'clusters' of abilities, experience and knowledge, and are frequently the things asked for in job advertizements. For example, an advert may demand leadership skills, creativity, persuasiveness and planning ability. If you want to know more about competencies, a list, with definitions, is provided in the Appendix to this book.

After the job analysis and the testing, the first step is to compare the results against the appropriate normative group. The findings can then be expressed in a number of ways, but one of the commonest is to describe the overall results in terms of percentiles. For example, if you score at the 70th percentile it means that you have done better than 70 per cent of the population; or, to put it another way, you are in the top 30 per cent.

The next step involves taking one of three approaches. The first approach is called 'top-down' selection. As the name implies this means that you select the top scorers, from the highest downwards, until you have filled all your positions. However, there can be problems, for example what happens if all the test takers actually got relatively low scores? In reality none of them may be particularly good prospects. Also, if you only select from the top scores, you might recruit people who are too high powered for the job in question. This is a real danger and was a mistake made in the 1980s by a number of major UK banks. The end result was a rapid and expensive turnover of staff as a result of their boredom.

An alternative approach is to use a 'minimum cut-off' technique. This relies on setting a minimum level for a test, or tests, above which candidates have to score. The level is usually established by testing existing employees, and is set at the point that represents satisfactory performance. But, as with the top-down approach, there can be difficulties, especially if the job is a new one. How can you set a standard for a job no one else is doing? It also relies on existing personnel being willing to be tested, and clearly on them actually being good performers in the first place! However, all other things being equal, this is still a very popular approach.

The last way of dealing with test results is to concentrate on profiles. What this means is that if a number of tests have been taken it is possible to look at the 'shape' of the results. In this way the psychologist or personnel manager can see the relative strengths and weaknesses of an applicant. For example, many administrative jobs require greater verbal and numerical ability than they do perceptual ability (understanding diagrams). This difference is obvious if the relative levels of test results are compared. Once this initial assessment is made the minimum requirements on individual tests can then be considered.

Example: selecting civil aviation pilots

In the United Kingdom, after applicants for pilot training have been pre-selected on the basis of their qualifications, age and interest in flying (which may include having a Private Pilots Licence), the next step is to complete a battery of tests called the Morrisby Profile. This involves 12 different tests that measure a range of different aptitudes and work-based personality. The results for each candidate are then compared with the ideal profile for the job.

The assessors look for good general reasoning ability, which is related to the ability to plan well; strong numerical and diagrammatic aptitude, with a slightly lower level of verbal aptitude, characteristic of those with technical ability; and a practical problem-solving style. In terms of personality, the best candidates are flexible and able to cope with change, possess a high degree of motivation and confidence, and are good team players.

After the results for each candidate have been analysed, candidates are graded into one of three categories: Grade 'A' for those who meet all the requirements, 'B' for those who meet most of the requirements, and 'C' for those who have serious weaknesses or who just have the 'wrong' sort of profile. When this is done it is not unusual to find that only 12–15 per cent make it into the 'A' category.

Obviously this is a very rigorous form of assessment, as would be expected when the responsibilities of a pilot are considered. It should also be noted that in this case the profile approach implies that effective pilots have, for example, good numerical and diagrammatic ability, but a lower level of verbal ability. This does not mean that verbal ability is not important, but rather that the other two general abilities are of greater importance in this instance.

The different sorts of abilities and personality characteristics that can be measured are explained in more detail in Chapters 3 and 6.

The profile approach is the most complex, but probably also the fairest of them all. However, as it takes more time than straight 'top-down' or 'minimum cut-off' approaches, it tends to be used less.

What influences test performance?

There are many techniques you can use to improve your test results, and these are covered in the chapters that follow. However, there are some factors you cannot control and that will inevitably influence how you perform in a test situation. These include things like age, gender and health, and also your educational, ethnic and home background.

As we get older some of our mental faculties tend to decline. For example, if you measure general intelligence you find that the peak ages are from about 15 years old to the mid-20s. After that it's downhill all the way! But before you get too depressed, this does not apply to all abilities, and general knowledge and experience increase with age. Personality also tends to stabilize with age, and the older you get the better you are at coping with your own personality.

Your gender can also influence your test performance. It's a fact that women do less well, on average, on tests of mechanical and spatial ability. These are tests that measure how good you are at understanding basic mechanical principles, and at imagining objects in three dimensions. However, to even up the balance, women frequently do better than men on tests of speed and accuracy. On average, this time, they are quicker and more precise in what they do.

If you are unwell at the time you do a test it will affect your performance. For example, if you have a temperature or just feel generally below par, it's unlikely that you will be able to do your best. Other long-lasting conditions such as anything affecting the movement of your hands, wrists and arms will also tend to interfere with your test-taking ability, especially how quickly you can work. This is important because many of the tests you will encounter will have strict time limits.

Aspects of where you come from, the standard of your education, your ethnic origin and your home environment can also influence how you do. For example, if you didn't do very well at school, or just didn't like it, it's probable that your results on attainment tests will be lower than they could be. Conversely, if you come from a home environment where study and reading were encouraged, this will probably increase your chances of getting better results.

Another very important factor is your ability with the English language. This can make a real difference because if

English is your second, or even your third, language, you will be at a disadvantage in most tests. The reason is that the vast majority of tests are only available in English, and if you have to think in your native language and then translate answers into English it will significantly slow your progress. The end result will be lower marks because tests operate within strict time limits.

In conclusion, what we are really talking about is opportunity, and if there are any factors that reduced your exposure to good education and learning, these will have an effect.

Key points

- A psychometric test is a standard and scientific way of assessing an aspect of human performance or behaviour.
- Tests measure things like general intelligence, attainment, aptitude and personality. They can also measure attitudes, interests, values and what motivates you.
- Tests are constructed so that they are objective, reliable, valid and unbiased. A great deal of effort is put into making them a fair way of assessing people.
- Tests results are used to assess people against the requirements for a job. Jobs are usually specified in terms of the knowledge, skills, abilities and the experience required to do them.
- Tests results are interpreted by comparing them against a standard group of people who have done the test in the past (the normative group).
- Decisions are made by applying one of a number of techniques. The most common approaches are 'top-down' and 'minimum cut-off' selection, or profiling.
- There are many factors that can influence your performance on a test. These include age, gender and health, and all aspects of your personal background.

2

Preparing for psychometric tests

When you apply for a job your application form or CV is compared against the requirements for that job. If you fulfil the initial requirements, in terms of things like qualifications and experience, you may then be asked to attend a test session. This session is designed to fill in some of the gaps, to provide additional information on your abilities and, more often than not, your personality.

The test session is usually scheduled for about 7–10 days after all the applications have been processed, and is marked by a letter of invitation. In the letter you will be told about the time and place of the session, how to get there, and any other points that might be important. Some employers will also include a practice test, which will explain why the test, or tests, are being used; how you might benefit from the testing process; and what the questions will look like. Indeed most practice tests include a number of questions for you to attempt and, of course, the answers. The purpose of practice tests is to give everyone an equal chance and, importantly, to give some practice material to those who have not done tests before.

A typical letter of invitation looks like this:

Mr D Grayson
12 Oak Tree Avenue
Longton
East Middleshire
EM12 4TX

[Date]

Dear Mr Grayson

Administration Manager Position

Thank you for applying for the position of Administration
Manager in our Holytown store. We have now assessed all
the applications and would like to invite you to a
psychometric testing session to be held at the Holytown
store on 18 May at 9:30 am. You will find a map and
details of car parking attached. If you are coming by
train the nearest station is Holytown Riverside, on the
Eastern Line.
The test session will last for two hours with a short
break in the middle. You will be asked to complete two
tests of ability, and a personality questionnaire. To
give you an idea of what to expect we have enclosed a
practice paper. If you read the instructions and answer
the questions it will help you understand what the tests
are measuring, and what the real test questions will look
like.
You do not need to bring any pens, writing materials, or
a pocket calculator to the test session, as everything
will be provided. However, if you normally wear reading
glasses make sure you bring them with you. Also, if you
are going to find it difficult to go for two hours
without anything to eat or drink, remember that there
will be a break in the middle when refreshments will be
provided.
Please let me know as soon as possible if you can attend
this session. If you have any questions contact my assistant, John Blake, on Holytown 339978. I look forward to
meeting you on 18 May.
Yours sincerely,

Jenny Munroe
Human Resources Manager
Triangle Stores Group

Coping with test anxiety

The prospect of being tested fills many people with anxiety. Indeed, even those who are used to formal tests and examinations are likely to suffer from at least some degree of nervousness. This is all perfectly natural and is a consequence of the importance of the situation, where a job may depend on your performance; and the unknown elements of the testing process. Practice tests, if they are used, are designed to help with the last point, but even so there is still room for the imagination to do its worst!

The first thing to appreciate is that a certain degree of anxiety actually improves performance. The trick is to manage it, and to make sure that it does not reach an unacceptable level. You will know if it's unacceptable because you will start to show some of the classic physical and behavioural signs of stress. These include the following.

Physical signs

- general fatigue;
- sleeplessness;
- headaches;
- back or shoulder ache;
- upset stomach.

Behavioural signs

- irritability;
- loss of concentration;
- depression;
- change in appetite (eating more *or* less than usual);
- drinking or smoking more;
- feelings of panic.

Before you get too worried, there are effective ways of controlling all of these stress symptoms. By far the best is to know what to expect, and this is what this chapter and the rest of the book is about. It's also important immediately to control unwanted and irrational thoughts, and to dismiss notions such as:

- Tests confuse me.
- My mind will go blank.
- I can never remember anything.
- I always go to pieces.
- I always run out of time.
- My memory will let me down.
- I'm stupid, I won't be able to do it...

As any counsellor or psychologist would point out, having these thoughts does not make them happen. They are just a reflection of the performance anxiety you feel before a test session. The key is to keep everything in proportion and not to start to believe what are frequently completely unrealistic personal 'predictions'. It's very unlikely to be a complete disaster, your family will not disown you; and if the worst comes to the worst, there are always other opportunities.

Practically, you need to get yourself into good mental and physical shape for a test session. This means getting enough sleep, eating and drinking properly, and making sure that you have taken enough exercise. If you're going to prepare for tests by working through practice questions or specialist books, do not stay up all night studying. Let's face it, it's very unlikely that you will do your best if you are tired, hungry and pumped full of caffeine!

You will also find it useful to build in periods of formal relaxation to your daily timetable. These may include any sort of activities that help you to unwind, and perhaps one of a number of special methods of stress reduction. Strategies such as these are important if you're presently unemployed and looking for a job, and also if you already have one and wish to move to a new position.

The two methods of stress reduction it is useful to know

about are simple body relaxation and visualization. Both these approaches have proven ability to reduce anxiety levels and to make taking tests a less stressful process. They can be practised in the days leading up to the test session, and while waiting to go in to the test room itself.

Simple body relaxation

This is a technique that will help you to relax your muscles in sequence from your feet to your head, taking in your legs, thighs, chest, shoulders, arms, neck and head. It's a classic method and is very effective in calming the body and reducing feelings of stress and anxiety. Interestingly, it is also a technique that is taught to people who want to learn about self-hypnosis. However, in saying this, do not worry about putting yourself into a trance. If you are tired to start with the most that will happen is that you will fall asleep.

The sequence of instructions is easy to remember and you can practise relaxing yourself at any time when you have 10 minutes or so to spare. All you need is a quiet room, which is at a comfortable temperature, where you are unlikely to be disturbed. Prior to a test session you can achieve the same results by sitting quietly with your eyes closed, silently working through the instructions in your head.

To relax your body, work through the following steps. Concentrate on your:

- **toes** – tense the muscles in your toes, and then relax;
- **feet** – tense the muscles in both your feet, and then relax;
- **lower legs** – tense your lower leg muscles, and then relax;
- **thighs** – tense your thigh muscles, and then relax;
- **stomach and lower back** – tense the muscles, and then relax;
- **chest** – tense the muscles in your chest, and then relax;
- **shoulders** – tense your shoulder muscles, and then relax;

- **upper arms** – tense the muscles in your upper arms, and then relax;
- **lower arms and hands** – tense all the muscles and then relax;
- **neck** – tense your neck muscles and then relax;
- **head** – tense your head muscles (frown!), and then relax.

If you follow this sequence you should feel a warm wave of relaxation spreading up your body. It should help you to feel comfortable and less anxious. If you only have time to follow a shorter sequence just concentrate on your shoulders, neck and head. Systematically tensing and relaxing just these muscle groups will make quite a difference. Finally, remember that if you want to try this technique immediately before a test session you can always use the washroom.

Visualization

This technique, also known as 'mental picturing', is designed to put you in a positive frame of mind. It's routinely used by sports professionals as it also has the effect of focusing the attention on the task at hand.

The idea is to put yourself into a daydream state and to imagine success. In this case you imagine the successful and satisfactory completion of a test session. It works because it has been found that repeatedly picturing something, clearly and vividly, acts on the unconscious mind. In fact the mind begins to believe the 'dream', and starts to mobilize resources to make it a reality. At the same time, because your mind is focused on a successful outcome, you do not have time to worry.

In order to use visualization to help you prepare for a test session you need to do the following:

- Make yourself comfortable. You can do this by using the progressive body relaxation technique described earlier. Alternatively you can just settle yourself down in a warm, quiet room and empty your mind of extraneous thoughts – try focusing on something in front of you, maybe a plant or an object, and letting any thoughts you have drift away.
- Check that you feel relaxed. Mentally run round your body and make sure that no particular part is feeling tense. If it is, concentrate on that part and relax the muscles.
- Think about a time when you were successful at something. Remember the feeling of success, the euphoria at having achieved something worthwhile. Imagine doing the same thing again, and the pleasant feelings that went with it. Try and visualize yourself passing that examination; winning the sports competition; signing the big contract – whatever has made you feel proud and successful. Hold on to the positive and warm thoughts you are having...
- Now visualize yourself waiting outside the test room feeling confident. You are well prepared, *you know what to expect*. You enter the room and sit in your place. On the table in front of you are some test books and answer papers, *as you anticipated*. You look around the room at the other candidates. You feel confident and know that you are just as well, if not better, prepared, than anyone else there. The test administrator introduces the session and *tells you what to expect*. The session starts and you carefully read the instructions for the first test. You have prepared yourself for this sort of test, and so you can immediately start on the first question. After the appropriate amount of time has passed the administrator asks you to stop. As you were told how long the test would last you have *budgeted your time accordingly*. More instructions follow, and you *complete* all the remaining tests and questionnaires. At the end of the session you know that you *understood the instructions for all of the tests, and completed every one to the best of your ability*. Hold on to that thought.

- Practise and follow the same pattern of thoughts in the days before the test session, and especially if you start to feel any nervousness or anxiety.

Both body relaxation and visualization only work if you practise. So think of them as new skills, and make sure that you put some effort into developing your techniques. They really can help you relax, and will put you in a winning frame of mind.

The test session

If you were expected to make any particular preparations before the test session these will have been outlined in your letter of invitation. However, it's probably worth mentioning at this point that if you have any special requirements you *must* make sure that the testing organization knows about them in advance. For example, if you have mobility problems ensure that provision has been made for you to get to the test room. If you have stiff or arthritic hands or wrists, tell them. Remember that many tests are timed and so you will not be able to work as quickly as other people. Also, if you have restricted eyesight, or hearing problems, make sure this is known. Larger print tests are available, and it is possible to 'reserve' a seat in the front row.

A test session is a formal event and so you can always expect the test administrator to explain exactly what is required. The following description covers the main features of *any* selection test administration, and concentrates on those things you need to consider in order to do your best.

In the test room

Tests take place in rooms with desks or tables laid out in rows, and at most sessions you will find yourself being tested with up to 20 other candidates. It is very unlikely that you will be tested by yourself, unless the test(s) are administered by computer.

In most test sessions it does not matter where you sit. However, if you are unsure, always ASK.

The test materials

When you sit down you will typically find a number of test question books, answer sheets, two pencils and an eraser in front of you. You will only be supplied with other items, rough paper or an electronic calculator, for example, if they are essential for any of the tests.

Use the materials provided. Do not use any pens or pencils you may have brought with you. The reason is that many test papers are marked by optical scanning systems, and these work best with pencil marks.

If the test materials do not comprise separate question books and answer sheets they will be in one of the following three formats:

1. A combined question and answer book that allows you to write your answers by the questions.
2. A question book and a 'palmtop' computer. In this arrangement you read the questions in the book and enter your answers using the computer keyboard.
3. A 'palm-top' or personal computer. This time the questions appear on the computer screen and you enter your answers using the keyboard.

There are also an increasing number of tests and questionnaires available via the internet. This means that it is possible for employers to sit you at a computer and present you with online assessments, taken directly from a website, or indeed from their own intranet.

The session introduction

When everyone is settled the test administrator (a personnel assistant, human resources (HR) manager or psychologist) will introduce the session. A typical introduction follows:

Good morning, I would first like to welcome you to The Triangles Stores Group – TSG. My name is Jenny Munroe and I am the Human Resources Manager with TSG. I will be organizing your activities this morning, and for the rest of your time with us.

Second, can I just check that you all received the details that we sent to you, and you know what is going to happen to you this morning. You should have received a practice test, which covered the verbal and numerical tests you will be completing, and some details on the personality questionnaire. Did you receive the details?

[Any questions are answered]

We use the tests described in your letter because they give a fair and objective view of your abilities and personality. We have found that people who do well on these tests also tend to do well in the job. However, I would just like to assure you that we do take other information into account, in particular your application details.

Before I introduce the tests themselves I would just like to make sure that you are all comfortable and ready to begin. Also, if you would like to visit the washroom, now is a good time. It's out of the door, turn left, through the double doors, and straight ahead. Are there any questions before we begin?

[There is a short break for visits to the washroom and questions]

The test session will last for two hours with a short break in the middle. There will be two tests of ability, verbal and numerical, and a personality questionnaire. I will tell you when to start and stop each test, so please do not open any of the booklets in front of you until you are told to begin.

In order to do your best you need to keep the following points in mind:

- Please ask questions *before* the tests if you do not understand what to do. I can always explain what you need to do again.
- Read the instructions for each test carefully. Don't rush as it's very important you complete the tests in the correct way.
- Work as quickly and as accurately as you can. Remember that there is a time limit for the tests.
- Don't spend too long on any question. If you can't do one, make an informed guess and go on with the next.
- Overall, the more questions you do, the better your chances of getting a higher score.

Do you have any final questions before we begin?

The tests

The administrator will read out the instructions for each test in turn. These will include details on how to approach the questions and the time allowed. You will also have an opportunity to complete some practice questions and ask any questions yourself.

Make sure you understand the practice questions. If you find them difficult, or just don't know what to do, ASK.

During the test session the administrator watches the candidates and records any events that may affect performance, eg excessive noise or disturbance. The administrator will also make a note if you ask for assistance or, for example, mark your answers on the wrong answer sheet. These factors will be taken into account at the marking stage. For instance, if you do put your answers on the wrong sheet, they will be transferred to the correct form and marked accordingly. It will not put you at a disadvantage.

The end of the session

At the end of the session the administrator will collect all the answer sheets, making sure that none is missing, and that they all have the candidates' names and other details on them. You will be thanked for attending and the next stage of the selection process will be explained. This will normally involve the scoring of the tests and the selection of people for interview.

In many cases tests can be marked very quickly and so interviews can take place on the same day as the testing. While this is happening your time may well be spent on a tour of the site or premises, or having lunch. After this period the 'successful' candidates will be invited to stay for interview.

If you are unsuccessful always ask if you can have some feedback on your test results.

A knowledge of your results will be invaluable for any further applications you make. Most companies are happy to give feedback, although it may only be at a later date and over the telephone. However, it's still going to be useful information about your test performance in a real selection situation.

Testing on the internet

Basically everything that applies to a paper-and-pencil test session also relates to one conducted via the internet. So either you will go to an employer's premises and the test will be administered automatically by computer, or you will be sent a link and be able to do the tests at home. And like paper-and-pencil tests there will be full instructions, example questions, practice items, and the whole session will be strictly timed.

It is interesting to note that online testing provides employers with a rich source of additional information, quite apart from the scores that you might obtain. For instance, the employer can quickly receive a highly comprehensive report on your abilities, or personality, which includes data on response patterns and timings. The latter can provide clues as to whether you were guessing or trying to answer according to some system; or, when it comes to time, those questions you were finding it difficult to understand.

As for sitting at home doing the tests, care is taken to ensure that individuals are issued with codes and asked to supply identifying information. This is to help to protect against someone else completing the tests for you! Also, it is worth bearing in mind that if you pass any online assessments you will probably be reassessed at the next stage of the selection process. All this means is that it is better to play by the rules.

Countdown to test-day

In the lead-up to a test session, make sure you learn as much as you can about the sort of tests or questionnaires you may be asked to complete. If you are sent a practice test make sure that you try it; and read any other details very carefully. It's also useful to work out exactly where you are expected to go for your tests, how you are going to get there, the time it will take, and so forth. There's nothing more unnerving than getting lost on the way and arriving late. Indeed, if you arrive very late you will not be able to take part in the test session.

T-DAY minus 7: the seven days before the test session

- Read all the materials that are sent to you with great care.
- Complete any practice tests supplied and check the answers.
- Use this book, and any other books containing practice questions, to prepare.
- Familiarize yourself with different sorts of test formats and questions.
- If you suffer from pre-test nerves try one of the relaxation techniques recommended earlier.
- Make sure you know *exactly* where, and at what time, the test session is being held.

T-DAY minus 1: the day before the test session

- Keep calm. If you've prepared yourself properly you don't need to panic.
- Review what you know about the tests you will be asked to complete.
- Reduce any tension by using a relaxation technique. Exercise is also a good way of reducing stress – try a brisk 20-minute walk.
- Eat normally. Don't overeat, or be tempted to drink a lot of alcohol, tea or coffee.
- Get a good night's sleep. Don't stay up all night 'cramming', or go out on a date!

T-DAY: the day of the test session

- Eat normally. Even if you don't feel like it have a decent breakfast. This is especially important if you're diabetic and suffer from low blood sugar.
- If you wear reading glasses or a hearing aid make sure you take them with you.
- Take the letter of invitation and the directions.
- Arrive at the test venue in good time. This means at least 15 to 20 minutes before the billed start time.
- Visit the washroom and have a quiet think.
- Make sure you know where to sit in the test room.

During the session

Here are 24 key points for test success:

1. Keep as calm as you can. Remember that a certain amount of anxiety is perfectly normal.
2. Don't show any agitation and don't lose your temper. You need to appear confident because your general behaviour will be under scrutiny as well as your test performance.

3. Make yourself comfortable. Loosen your collar and tie (if appropriate), and kick off your shoes if you need to.
4. Listen carefully to the administrator's instructions. Ask questions if you do not understand something.
5. If you can't see or hear things properly tell the administrator.
6. Read the test instructions carefully and do not assume that you know what to do.
7. Put your answers in the correct place on the answer sheet. If you miss a question out, because you intend to return to it, make sure you do not get out of sequence. Of course with computer or online testing the system will make sure that you are answering the right question. Most will also allow you to go back and change answers, within the time limits of the test.
8. Record your answers in the correct way. For example, do not tick boxes if you're expected to strike through them with short pencil lines.
9. Read the questions properly before you attempt to answer them.
10. Don't agonize over a question you can't do, but move on to the next one.
11. Don't waste time double-checking questions with easy or obvious answers.
12. Don't waste time looking for 'trick' questions as there won't be any.
13. If you can't work out an answer, make an informed guess.
14. Work as quickly as you can, but don't race or you will make avoidable mistakes. For example, it's very easy to reverse numbers and to imagine, say, that an answer is 145 rather than 154.
15. Remember that the more questions you answer the greater your chances of getting a higher mark.
16. Keep an eye on the time. If you have time left at the end of a test go back and check your answers. Computer or online tests will provide an on-screen clock. This will count down the time to the end of the test.

17. Don't stick slavishly to a certain amount of time for each question, eg 30 seconds for each question, if there are 60 to complete in half-an-hour. Many tests are designed so that the questions get harder, and so need progressively more time as you go on.

18. If you want any assistance during a test ask the administrator. The administrator won't give you further instructions once the test has started, but will be able to help you with any problems you might have concerning the 'mechanics' of the session, eg not knowing where to write your answers, a defective question book, blunt or broken pencils, no eraser...

19. Look around occasionally and relax: take some deep breaths, rest your eyes, stretch your legs. This will help to break the tension that will inevitably build up in your body.

20. Don't be put off if the questions seem difficult. They may well be just as difficult for everyone else, and you don't know the pass mark.

21. Don't be alarmed if your neighbours appear to be working much quicker than you. It's no guarantee that their answers are correct!

22. If for any reason you feel unwell tell the administrator. There are no prizes for suffering in silence. This applies to online tests as well. If something happens during the test session, or if you feel ill, contact the administrator by telephone after the session.

23. Don't be hard on yourself, you can only do your best.

24. Keep a cool head and, if you need help, ask for it.

3

Ability tests

There are about 50 human abilities that can be measured using psychometric tests. These fall into four main categories covering the cognitive abilities such as numerical or verbal reasoning; psychomotor abilities like hand–eye co-ordination; physical abilities relating to stamina and strength; and sensory abilities concerning vision, hearing and speech.

In an assessment context the tests used may be selected from just one of these categories, or from a number. For example, some jobs require verbal and numerical ability; while others demand numerical and perceptual reasoning (understanding diagrams) *and* perfect colour vision. So the task of the personnel specialist can be very complicated because different jobs require different tests, and also because there is a vast range of tests to choose from. In fact there are between 4,000 and 5,000 tests on the market, with virtually all of them designed for use in English-speaking countries.

This makes the job of preparing for ability tests sound rather overwhelming, but in reality most selection procedures focus on the six main types of cognitive reasoning test:

● abstract;
● verbal;
● numerical;
● perceptual;

- spatial;
- mechanical.

There are other sorts of cognitive tests such as those that assess the ability to check information quickly and accurately. This is an important ability to measure in any job requiring the processing of large quantities of detailed information.

The next section deals with the six main types and provides information on what is being measured, the different sorts of question format, and hints on improving your performance. There is also some guidance on which type and format of test is used to assess which sort of job, along with the names of some of the most commonly used tests.

Abstract reasoning

Abstract reasoning tests measure general intellectual reasoning ability. This concerns how well you can solve a problem from first principles. It involves identifying the underlying logic of an 'argument' or question.

The questions in this sort of test are usually in the form of sequences of symbols arranged in rows or squares, and in order to solve them you must work through three distinct steps: your first task is to identify the different sorts of symbols, and decide what they have in common. For example, in most tests the differences will include some or all of the following:

- **shape,** eg circles, triangles, squares, rectangles, pentagons, hexagons;
- **size,** eg small, medium and large;
- **colour,** eg the three primary colours;
- **features,** eg the number of circles, lines or points on a star.

Having examined the symbols, and what they have in common, the next step is to identify the pattern. This involves seeing how the symbols are ordered or grouped. For example, are they in repeating patterns of two, three or more symbols? If they are in a square format, does the order go from left to right, right to left, top to bottom, bottom to top, or diagonally?

The last step is to predict the next part of the sequence from what you have learnt about the logic of the pattern.

Example 1: Abstract Reasoning
What are the next two symbols in the sequence?

Example 2: Abstract Reasoning
What is the missing symbol?

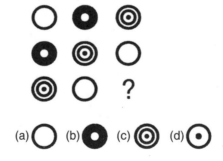

In Example 1 you will see that there are four different types of symbol, all of which are the same size. The (a) symbol always goes immediately after the (d) symbol, leaving the other two to alternate. Since there are two (b)s and only one (c), the next symbols in the sequence must be (c), followed by (d). Likewise in Example 2, it's a question of working out what is happening in each row or column. This one is obviously easier because there are three symbols in use, and they appear in each complete row or column only once. Thus it is logical to assume that the missing symbol is (b). However, it's also interesting to note that there is a sequence, which runs (a)–(c)–(b). This is an important point to grasp because in questions presented as 'squares' there is often more than one way of reaching the correct answer.

Uses

Abstract reasoning tests provide the best single measure of general ability and so are used for all types of jobs at all levels. This means that there is a chance you will have to do this sort of test whatever the job for which you are applying. However, they are obviously of particular value for any job that focuses on the ability to deal with abstract ideas, concepts or theories. Thus they are generally a fixed feature of recruitment to scientific or technological jobs.

The most widely used tests of general intellectual ability are *Raven's Progressive Matrices*, published by Oxford Psychologists Press. Another popular measure is the *Compound Series Test* from The Morrisby Organization.

Hints

Seek out abstract problems in newspapers, magazines and quiz books, and practise working through the three steps suggested. You may also find it useful to make up your own questions and try them on other people. The action of explaining the answers will help fix in your mind the different ways in which these questions can work. Finally, if you get stuck on a particular question in a test, always go back to first principles and identify the component parts of the symbols, and then the pattern. Sometimes it also helps to continue with the other questions and return to a problem question later with a fresh viewpoint. This will stop you becoming fixated on a particular solution.

Verbal reasoning

Verbal reasoning tests measure your ability to understand and use words. They are concerned with things like spelling, grammar, sentence completion, analogies and following verbal instructions. The more complex verbal tests look at how well you can understand and reason with passages of verbal information. The questions in verbal tests come in many different forms, but they all rely on understanding the meaning of words, and the structure and logic of language.

Example 3: Spelling
Which of the following words are *incorrectly* spelt?
(a) Persistant (b) Separate (c) Success (d) Recieve

Example 4: Grammar
What, if anything, is grammatically *incorrect* with the following sentences?
(a) The elephant was very enormous.
(b) Its unlikely that we can catch the train.
(c) She took the books and the rest of the money off of me.
(d) They should have took the boxes with them.

Example 5: Sentence Completion
Which word best completes the sentence?
1.   The painting, originally .... to a Dutch artist, is now thought to be by John Constable.
(a) prescribed (b) assigned (c) attributed (d) linked
(e) designated
2.   Our company's name is .... with quality and value for money.
(a) connected (b) synonymous (c) aligned (d) concerned
(e) equated

In Example 3 you need to know how to spell a series of everyday words, and (a) and (d) are incorrectly spelt. The trick with Example 4 is to understand some of the principles of

English grammar, and to realize that there are errors in all of them! In (a) the word 'very' is not needed, as 'enormous' means 'very large'; in (b), 'Its' should be 'It's'; and in (c) the word 'of' is not required. Finally, in (d), the word 'took' should be 'taken'. In Example 5 the questions are known as 'cloze' tasks, and the idea in each case is to identify the best possible word. Therefore in question (1) the most correct answer is (c), because paintings are 'attributed' to artists; and in (2) the answer is (b), because 'synonymous' means 'closely associated'.

Example 6: Verbal Analogies
Letter is to word as sentence is to:
(a) verb (b) paragraph (c) phrase (d) book
Over is to under as below is to:
(a) beneath (b) beside (c) above (d) submerged

Example 7: Word Groups
Which *two* words do not belong with the other four?
1. (a) stone (b) wood (c) plastic (d) coal (e) nylon (f) gas
2. (a) trousers (b) hat (c) socks (d) shirt (e) boots (f) shorts

Example 8: Following Instructions
Use the information below to answer the questions. For each question select the correct answer from the five options provided.

Surgery Times
The surgery is now open from 8.30 am to 12.30 pm, and from 1.00 pm to 6.30 pm.

There is a late surgery on Tuesdays and Thursdays from 7.30 pm to 10.00 pm. If you have a minor surgery appointment please confirm at the beginning of the week, as all procedures are performed on Thursday afternoons. The 'Well Woman' clinic continues to take place on alternate Saturday mornings. The next meeting is scheduled for the 25th of this month, please see the practice nurse for details.

If you have a minor surgery appointment when must you attend?

(a) Normal surgery hours.
(b) Late surgery on Thursday.
(c) The beginning of the week.
(d) Monday or Wednesday morning.
(e) Thursday afternoon.

In Examples 6 and 7 you need to understand directly the meanings and relationships between words. Thus, in Example 6, the answer to the first analogy is (b), because the progression is to bigger units; and in the other analogy the answer is (c) because the starting analogy was one of opposites. Readers should note that in this sort of question there may be *any* relationship between the words, eg:

● **synonyms,** ie words with the same meanings;
● **antonyms,** ie words with opposite meanings;
● **part to whole,** eg 'letter' is to 'word';
● **cause and effect,** eg 'exercise' is to 'fatigue';
● **sequence,** eg 'summer' is to 'autumn';
● **degree,** eg 'hot' is to 'warm';
● **object and action,** eg 'kick' is to 'football';
● **groups,** eg 'red' is to 'green' (other colours).

Indeed, Example 7 is a case of words falling into particular groups. So the answer to (1) is (c) and (e) because they are both man-made, while the other materials are natural; and to (2) it is (b) and (d), because they are items of clothing worn above the waist, while the others are worn below. In Example 8 details are given of a doctor's surgery times and the question is designed to discover whether you can understand simple instructions. The answer is actually very straightforward and is (e). However, these sorts of questions can be much more difficult, eg on what date was the last 'Well Woman' clinic?

The most complicated sorts of verbal assessments are called

verbal critical reasoning tests. These present you with a short passage of written information followed by a number of statements. The task is to decide whether each statement is 'True' (follows logically from the information provided); 'False' (does not follow logically); or if you 'Cannot Tell', because there is insufficient information. All the information required to make the decision is contained in the passage. However, just to complicate the issue, the information given frequently relates to subjects about which you may already know, or have formed particular opinions about.

Example 9: Verbal Critical Reasoning
Read the passage and decide if the statements that follow are True, False or if you Cannot Tell.

'Smoking can cause problems in many work environments. In the office it can not only lead to heated arguments, but to health problems as well. Indeed the *New England Journal of Medicine* (NEJM) recently reported that passive smoking, or the involuntary inhalation of other people's smoke, can be a major health hazard. Like regular smokers, it puts passive smokers at an increased risk of developing chest and circulatory diseases.'

1. Smokers are more likely to have heart attacks.
2. Passive smoking means inhaling someone else's smoke.
3. Smoking can make offices calmer places in which to work.

Some verbal critical reasoning tests have more than three answer options, and split the reasoning tasks into a number of types. So, for example, you have to decide if a statement is 'True', 'Probably True', 'False', 'Probably False' or if you 'Cannot Tell'. The questions are then based on different types of logical argument, eg:

● whether deductions (judgements based on general principles) are valid;

- whether inferences (conclusions based on given facts) are accurate;
- whether valid assumptions are being made;
- the strength of verbal arguments;
- whether conclusions based on factual interpretations are valid.

For example, deductions are sometimes based on pairs of logically consistent verbal arguments or 'syllogisms'.

Example 10: Verbal Deductions
'Some animals are venomous. All venomous animals are dangerous to touch.'

Which of the following are valid deductions?

1. All non-venomous animals are safe to touch.
2. Some animals are dangerous.
3. Some animals are safe to touch.

The answers to Example 9 are (1), 'Cannot Tell'; (2) 'True'; and (3) 'False'. If you made a mistake it's probably because you allowed your opinions or existing knowledge to cloud your judgement. Thus it is well known that smoking increases your chances of having a heart attack, but the necessary information is not provided in the passage. In a similar way in Example 10 you have to be careful what you assume. The answer to (1) is 'No', because we have no information on non-venomous animals, and some may be dangerous. The answer to (2) is 'Yes', because according to the statements the animals that are venomous are dangerous to touch. Finally, the answer to (3) is 'No' again, because although we know there are animals that are safe to touch, we have no given information on which to base that conclusion.

Uses

Verbal reasoning tests are probably the most widely used type of ability measure. They are popular with employers because every job requires the ability to assess and use verbal information, whether it be understanding instruction manuals or writing management reports. In practice the formats illustrated by Examples 3 to 8 tend to be used in selection for semi-skilled, general administrative, clerical and customer service positions, whereas the verbal critical reasoning tests (Examples 9 and 10) are generally used for managerial and graduate selection.

There are many verbal tests on the market including *Working with Words, Verbal Comprehension, Verbal Usage, Verbal Reasoning, Verbal Analysis* and *Verbal Critical Reasoning* from Saville & Holdsworth Ltd. Other examples include the verbal component of the *Graduate and Managerial Assessment* and *First Graduate Assessment*, published by ASE; and the *Watson Glaser Critical Thinking Appraisal* from The Psychological Corporation.

Hints

A good way to prepare for verbal tests is to read and analyse complex verbal information. Try reading a quality newspaper and deciding if the assertions and assumptions made by the journalists are supported by the facts. You might also find it useful to read manuals and technical reports, and 'test' them for the logic of their arguments.

Other things to try are word games like Scrabble and the verbal logic puzzles you find in puzzle books available from newsagents. You must also attempt to expand your word power by reading more, and looking up any words you do not understand in a dictionary. A thesaurus, available from any good bookshop, will also be a useful addition to your library as it contains lists of synonyms and antonyms.

On a more technical note, when you are reading the questions in a verbal test it's worth remembering that if you read all the possible answers carefully, they will often give you clues as to the correct response. For example:

- the correct response is often shorter and more detailed;
- information given in the other answers may help to identify the correct response;
- the incorrect answers are often inconsistent or implausible;
- the use of absolutes (eg 'every', 'all') often appear in false statements.

Numerical reasoning

Numerical reasoning tests measure your ability to understand and use numbers. They are concerned with the four basic arithmetic operations (addition, subtraction, multiplication and division), number sequences, simple mathematics and the use of numerical data to solve problems. The latter is usually the case with numerical critical reasoning tests in which blocks of information are provided that require both interpretation and the application of the appropriate logic.

Example 11: Arithmetic
Solve *without* a calculator.

1.	24.7 × 4 = ?	(a) 84.3	(b) 89.8	(c) 92.3	(d) 96.7	(e) 98.8
2.	719 + ? = 866	(a) 156	(b) 142	(c) 177	(d) 147	(e) 158
3.	? − 48 = 112	(a) 152	(b) 162	(c) 154	(d) 160	(e) 149
4.	24.6 ÷ 5.3 = ?	(a) 3.7	(b) 4.2	(c) 4.6	(d) 5.1	(e) 5.4

Example 12: Number Sequences
What is the next number in the sequence?

1.	1	4	7	10	13	16	?
2.	3	9	27	81	243	729	?
3.	1	4	9	16	25	36	?
4.	1	1	2	3	5	8	?

Example 13: Mathematics
Solve *without* a calculator.

1.	25% of 500 = ?	(a) 120	(b) 250	(c) 125	(d) 220	(e) 175
2.	3x + 12 = 18, x =	(a) 2	(b) 2.5	(c) 3	(d) 3.5	(e) 4
3.	(7 × 6) + ? = 70	(a) 38	(b) 32	(c) 18	(d) 42	(e) 28
4.	1/6 as a decimal	(a) 0.155	(b) 0.333	(c) 0.225	(d) 0.166	(e) 0.175

The answers to Example 11 are (e), (d), (d) and (c). Note that it's often a lot easier to work out the answer if you round the numbers, eg in question 1 if you look for the answer that is nearest to 25 × 4. In Example 12 the answer to 1 is 19, because the difference between each number and the preceding one is 3. Sequences like this, where you add or subtract a fixed number, are known as arithmetic progressions. In 2 the answer is 2187, because the next number is always found by multiplying the preceding number by 3. This is an example of a geometric progression. In 3 the answer is 49, because all the numbers are squares (1 × 1, 2 × 2, 3 × 3, 4 × 4, 5 × 5, 6 × 6, 7 × 7). In 4 the answer is 13, because the next number is the last two numbers added together. For the mathematically minded this is an example of what is known as the Fibonacci sequence. All these types of sequences are frequently used in numerical tests.

In Example 13 you need to go beyond simple arithmetic and understand how percentages work, simple algebra, the meaning of brackets and how to convert to decimal fractions. The answers are (c), (a), (e) and (d). All these mathematical operations are based on the sort of things you learn in secondary education.

Numerical critical reasoning tests present you with a range of numerical information, usually in the form of tables of data, charts or graphs. The task is to understand the meaning of the questions, find and interpret the appropriate data, and then perform the necessary calculations. In most cases the calculations are not difficult and the emphasis is on developing the correct problem-solving strategy. In this way, although the problems can seem complicated, they do not usually require a calculator. Indeed in most tests of this nature candidates are not allowed to use calculators.

Example 14: Numerical Critical Reasoning
Use the information below to answer the questions.

STUDENT EXAMINATION PERFORMANCE

Qualifications by Level and Gender

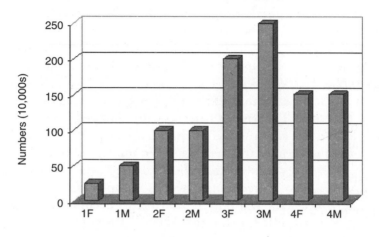

College Qualifications by Level

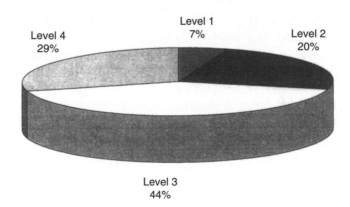

Key: Educational Levels are 1–4. Gender: M = Male and F = Female.

Questions:
1. How many women have Level 3 qualifications?
(a) 250,000   (b) 200,000   (c) 2,000,000   (d) 2,500,000
2. What percentage of students have Level 2 or better qualifications?
(a) 93%   (b) 83%   (c) 63%   (d) 73%
3. If the ratio of males to females with Level 4 qualifications is kept constant, but these qualifications make up 39% of the total, approximately how many more students will now have Level 4 qualifications?
(a) 250,000   (b) 500,000   (c) 750,000   (d) 1,000,000

The Example 14 questions are quite typical of numerical critical reasoning tests as they involve the use of one or more charts and then a calculation. As you can see it is important to understand how the charts are labelled, in particular that the 'Qualifications by Level and Gender' chart has a scale marked in 10,000s. The answer to question 1 is obtained by reading off the value and multiplying it by 10,000, which gives (c). Question 2 relates to the pie chart with the answer being (a). Lastly, there are a number of ways of working out the answer to question 3, but if 29 per cent is equal to three million then 39 per cent must be equal to about four million. This gives a difference of one million, which is answer (d).

Uses

Numerical tests, especially those based on question formats like Examples 11 to 13, are used in selection whenever there is a need to assess numeracy or an aptitude for data manipulation. This covers many clerical and administrative jobs, as well as those in the banking and financial services sector. Graduates and managerial applicants can look forward to completing numerical critical reasoning tests with questions like those in Example 14.

As numerical reasoning tests are so commonly used there are

many to choose from. In the UK the most popular include *Working with Numbers*, *Number Skills*, *Numerical Computation*, *Numerical Reasoning*, *Numerical Estimation*, *Interpreting Data*, *Numerical Analysis* and *Numerical Critical Reasoning*, all published by Saville & Holdsworth Limited. Other names to look out for are *Numerical Awareness* and *Numerical Estimation* (*Modern Occupational Skills Tests*), and the numerical component of the *Graduate and Managerial Assessment* and *First Graduate Assessment*, all published by ASE.

Hints

Make sure you are capable of performing simple calculations without a calculator. You can practise these when you go shopping by working out how much you will need to pay for your purchases, the real cost of discounted goods, the cost per minute of leaving your car in a car park and so forth. It's also a good idea to practise with tables of information such as bus or train timetables, tables of currency exchange rates and the financial information contained in newspapers.

In terms of mathematical knowledge you will find it useful to understand:

● factors and multiples, eg powers and roots of numbers;
● fractions, ratios, proportions and percentages;
● different types of graphs, eg bar charts, pie charts and line graphs;
● simple statistics, eg how to work with frequencies or calculate an average.

If you are unsure about any of these aspects of mathematics consult a textbook, especially any general text covering GCSE or equivalent level maths.

Perceptual reasoning

Perceptual reasoning is about understanding and applying information presented in a diagrammatic form. Most tests of this nature are based on perceptual analogies, or involve the interpretation of diagrammatic rules. In both cases the answers can only be worked out by determining the visual logic of the information provided. Indeed they are deliberately designed so that a visual problem-solving strategy will work better than any other approach.

Example 15: Perceptual Analogies

1. ← is to → as: (a) ↑ (b) ↗ (c) ↙ is to (d) ↘ (e) ↓ (f) ↖

2. 🕙 is to 🕙 as: (a) 🕡 (b) 🕘 (c) 🕝 is to (d) 🕛 (e) 🕗 (f) 🕝

Example 16: Diagrammatic Interpretation
The following commands have the effects shown:

Command 1: ♥ ⇨ ▲   Command 4: ▼ ⇨ ♥

Command 2: ▼ ⇨ ▼   Command 5: ▲ ⇨ ■

Command 3: ■ ⇨ ♥   Command 6: ♥ ⇨ ▼

What will happen to the shape if the commands are applied?

A. ■⇨ 3⇨ 6 ⇨ 4 ⇨ ?   (a) ■ (b) ▼ (c) ♥ (d) ▲

B. ♥⇨ 6⇨ 4 ⇨ 1 ⇨ 5⇨ ? (a) ▲ (b) ♥ (c) ▼ (d) ■

C. ▲⇨ 2⇨ 4 ⇨ 6 ⇨ ?   (a) ■ (b) ▼ (c) ♥ (d) ▲

In Example 15, analogy 1 is a simple case of the different orientations of an arrow. The answer can only be worked out visually and is (a) and (e). In 2 you are presented with a series of clock faces, and the answer this time is (b) and (d). The quickest way to the solution is to realize that the difference between the two starting clocks is that the hour hand has rotated through 180 degrees, and to look for two other clock faces where this has happened. In Example 16 you are forced to imagine what will happen to a shape when it is transformed in various ways. Again this can only be done visually, and the answers are (c), (d) and (b).

Uses

Perceptual tests are often used to select for scientific, computing, engineering, design and technical craft positions. As with verbal and numerical tests they are also good predictors of performance in general managerial, administrative and office-based jobs. The same designs of tests are used with candidates applying for jobs at all levels. However, the tests can be made more complicated by introducing additional variables, eg in Example 16 there could have been additional commands that changed the size of the shapes, the colour, or which only worked in combination with other commands.

A classic example of a perceptual reasoning test is the *Perceptual Test* (part of the *General Ability Tests*), published by The Morrisby Organization. Others include the *Diagrammatic Reasoning* and *Diagrammatic Thinking* tests from Saville & Holdsworth Ltd.

Hints

The best form of practice for perceptual analogies is to buy a book containing plenty of examples and to work out the relationships between the shapes or diagrams. You will discover that the relationships you find are similar to those used in abstract reasoning tests, and some verbal analogies. They will include changes in size, colour or orientation; and the membership of groups of shapes, which get progressively more complicated, but which share similar features.

For tests based on diagrammatic interpretation, practise by producing your own diagrams that explain how a system works, eg draw a flow diagram which explains how to programme a video recorder. Any game involving sequences of moves can also be good practice; this would include any board game based on strategy.

Spatial reasoning

Spatial reasoning tests measure your ability to manipulate shapes in two dimensions, or to visualize solid objects presented as two-dimensional patterns. In the first case the test often presents you with a pattern that has some missing components, and you have to decide which of a number of alternate pieces will complete the pattern, or maybe just how many pieces are required. Other tests present two-dimensional objects that have been rotated or reflected, and you have to decide what has happened, eg whether or not a shape has been turned over. In those tests requiring the visualization of a solid object, a number of patterns are presented that could be folded to make an object. Your job is to imagine which of the patterns would work in practice.

All spatial tests rely on you being able to imagine what would happen 'in your mind's eye'. This is something that many people find difficult to do, and some cannot do it at all. Thus, about 5 per cent of the adult population will find it impossible to imagine a two-dimensional shape moved through a third dimension. Psychologically speaking this is an interesting finding as it probably means that spatial ability is something that gets wired into the brain quite early in life or, at the very least, by the end of the teenage years.

Example 17: Spatial Components

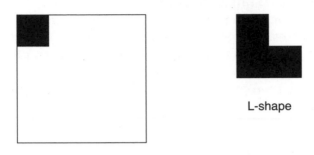

L-shape

How many of the L-shapes are required to fill the large square, without leaving any gaps?

(a) 3   (b) 4   (c) 5   (d) 6   (e) Cannot be done

Example 18: Spatial Rotations and Reflections
All of the shapes below are the same, but they have been rotated into different positions. In addition *one* of them has been turned over, which one?

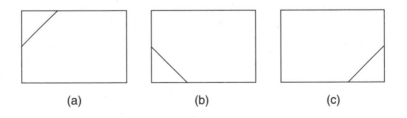

(a)   (b)   (c)

In Example 17 you will find that there is only one way of completing the square without leaving any gaps and this requires five of the L-shaped pieces – answer (c). The solution is to fit one piece around the black square in the top left-hand corner so that you end up with a complete small square, and then to fit two further L-shapes on the corner of that square so that you complete a diagonal going from the top left to bottom right. The remaining gaps are both L-shaped, and require two further pieces. The best way to work out the answer to Example 18 is to look for the one shape that has been turned over like the page of a book. Alternatively, you could look for two shapes, which when rotated will sit exactly on top of each other, making the remaining shape the one that has been turned over. Whichever strategy you use you should get (b) as the answer.

The last example measures advanced spatial reasoning and requires the ability to imagine patterns assembled into three-dimensional objects. Questions like this can involve the visual 'assembly' and 'disassembly' of objects; objects that have been rotated in space, or which are viewed from different angles (eg from above, below, the side, the back); and objects that have different colours or markings on their surfaces. The last variety are the hardest to deal with as they require an ability to imagine shapes moved in three-dimensional space, *and* the ability to work out the relative position of the markings on their surfaces.

Example 19: Spatial Assembly

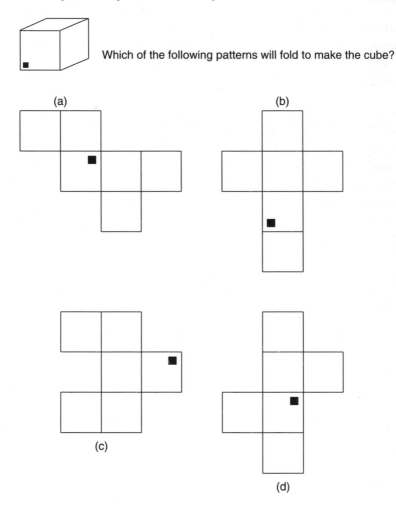

Which of the following patterns will fold to make the cube?

In order to answer Example 19 you first need to establish which of the patterns will fold to make the cube, and then which will have the small black square in the correct position. If you look at the patterns carefully you will see that (a), (b) and (d) will all fold to make a cube. In this case they will also all produce the cube illustrated.

Uses

Spatial reasoning tests are used in selection for jobs where it is necessary to have a good eye for how things fit together, or to be able to cope with different shapes and patterns. This includes many practical jobs such as carpentry, decorating, floor-laying and sewing. Good spatial ability is also required in many production, technical and design activities where plans and drawings are used extensively. Thus, you would expect surveyors, architects, engineers and designers to have this sort of ability. It is also an ability that can be used in conjunction with modern 'visualization' tools such as computer-aided design (CAD) packages.

Spatial reasoning tests are used less frequently than the other sorts of tests mentioned so far, but they do measure an ability that is a key component of many jobs. The tests on the market include the *Shapes Analysis Test*, published by The Test Agency; and the *Shapes Test*, from The Morrisby Organization. Other frequently used examples are the *Spatial Reasoning* and *Spatial Recognition* tests from Saville & Holdsworth Ltd.

Hints

Spatial reasoning is a very practical sort of ability and so it is best practised by assembling and making things. For example, you could build models or assemble jigsaw puzzles. In fact these days there are three-dimensional puzzles that provide very good practice in imagining how complex parts fit together. If you are artistic you can also try drawing plans of objects from different angles, or try cutting out and assembling the sort of patterns illustrated in Example 19. Finally, if you have access to a computer drawing or CAD package you can draw objects that you can instruct the computer to move in three-dimensional space. This will allow you to see objects in any orientation and from any angle.

Mechanical reasoning

Mechanical reasoning tests are designed to assess your knowledge of basic mechanical and physical principles. They usually contain questions that do not require any specialist knowledge, but which rely on you being able to work out what is happening. However, that's not to say that some knowledge of physics or mechanics, or practical everyday experience of simple machines and devices, would not be of help.

Example 20: Mechanical Reasoning

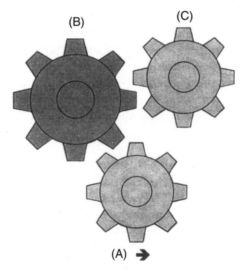

In which direction will C turn if A turns anti-clockwise?
(a) Clockwise   (b) It will jam   (c) Anti-clockwise
(d) Backwards and forwards

In virtually all mechanical reasoning tests you are presented with a question and a diagram. You have to determine what principle is being illustrated and select the correct answer from the options provided.

The answer to Example 20 is determined by imagining the effect of A on B, and then of B on C. In this way, even in this straightforward example, it involves step-by-step problem solving. If you approach the task in this way you will find that (c) is the correct answer. Looking at the other options, obviously (d) is incorrect, and so is (b). If you were tempted to answer (b) you were adding additional information to the diagram, eg by thinking that the cogs were too close together, or that friction would stop them turning. This is a common mistake with mechanical questions that can only be answered on the basis of the information provided, even if you think you know better!

Uses

Mechanical reasoning tests are used to assess people for practical jobs requiring a working knowledge of mechanical principles. These are often positions that involve assembling components or running and maintaining machinery. As a consequence, mechanical tests are often used to select mechanics, technicians and production workers.

One of the best-known mechanical reasoning tests is *Bennett's Mechanical Comprehension Test*, published by The Psychological Corporation. This was developed in the 1940s, and is still widely used throughout the world. Other more modern tests include the *Mechanical Test* from The Morrisby Organization and *Mechanical Comprehension* from Saville & Holdsworth Ltd.

Hints

If you are interested in maintaining any form of machine, including a motor car, you are probably already practising this ability. Likewise, if you undertake 'do-it-yourself' projects, or repair things around the home, you are giving yourself scope to exercise your mechanical competence. Other things you can do are to work with construction kits (eg Technical Lego or

Meccano); or simply to take household devices apart and put them back together again.

Research has shown that men are generally better at mechanical reasoning tests than women, so if you are female it's even more important that you understand the principles involved. However, whatever your gender, useful additional sources of information are GCSE level physics or technology textbooks. You will find that these give details on:

- **mechanisms**, eg balances, levers, linkages, gears, cranks and pulleys;
- **structures**, eg the effects of compression, stress and strain;
- **energy**, eg the transmission of heat, light and power;
- **forces**, eg gravity, and rotational effects such as centrifugal and centripetal force.

Other ability tests

The other main types of cognitive ability tests that you might encounter are concerned with checking detailed information. These are known as checking, data checking or classification tests. They are generally short in duration and present you with a number of tables of information, which you have to check against each other. The function of this sort of test is to measure how quickly and accurately you can detect errors in data. This is an ability that is important in any job where detailed records are kept, eg banking, accounting, telephone sales and retailing.

Example 21: Data Checking

Look at the two tables of data below. Check each row and mark any differences you find between Table A and Table B.

Table A				Table B		
Code	Number	Band		Code	Number	Band
127/34	2510	XA		127/34	2510	XA
128/35	2505	LM		128/53	2505	LM
129/36	2543	BA		129/36	2534	AB
218/43	3671	LM		218/43	3671	LM
218/44	3762	AB		218/44	3762	AB
219/45	3892	XA		219/54	3892	XA

In Example 21 there are differences in three of the rows. However, consider how much more difficult this test would be if there were 40 rows and 6 columns per table; and a mixture of numbers, letters, numbers and letters, and names and addresses – all to be checked in a matter of minutes.

Uses

As already mentioned, this sort of test is used to select people for clerical checking and data input jobs. Most of the major publishers produce tests that are a variation on the theme illustrated; with the *Speed and Accuracy Test* from The Morrisby Organization and *Clerical Checking* from Saville & Holdsworth Ltd being good examples.

Hints

Data checking tests require an eye for detail and patience. One way to practise is to cross-reference codes and other details in catalogues and timetables, or to check accounts or balance sheets. In short, use any form of detailed information that you can check for its accuracy.

Manual dexterity tests

Finally, if you apply for jobs that require speed and accuracy with the hands, you may be asked to take a manual dexterity test. These are often in the form of wooden pegboards on which you are asked to place combinations of metal pins and washers in holes. Sometimes there are a series of tasks to complete in different ways, such as just using your left or right hand, both hands, or a pair of tweezers. More complex forms of dexterity test may require you to assemble a number of different types of components in a given time. These often look like construction kits, and involve the use of your hands and some tools. Commonly used dexterity tests include the *Peg Board* and *Fine Dexterity Tests*, both available from The Morrisby Organization and the Test Agency.

Future test developments

In the short term you are likely to encounter more tests based on so-called business learning experiences. These are work simulation exercises in which you take the role of an employee in a fictional company or organization. The tests work by teaching you what you need to know in order to complete a range of tasks, and then by finding out how good you are at applying your learning in practice. A typical scenario might be that you have just taken over a customer service desk, and your supervisor has briefly introduced you to the product and customer databases, and to a procedures manual. Your first customer arrives with a query...

Business learning exercises differ from traditional tests, which measure specific abilities, in that they present complete problem scenarios. In this way they present more realistic problems, and allow an employer to see more directly how you would perform in a real job. Arguably, these exercises are a fairer method of selection because they make no assumptions about your existing knowledge and, also, because they sample real job situations, they allow for a degree of self-selection. The last point is important because it saves time for employer and candidate alike.

Over the next few years more of these tests will be used, in particular for selecting potential middle and senior managers, and customer service and sales personnel. The pioneers in this area are Oxford Psychologists Press, who publish tests such as the *Aptitude for Business Learning Exercises (ABLE)*.

Example 22: Business Learning Exercise

Instructions

You have just started a job in the marketing department of a large travel group. Your first task is to update some new holiday brochures. This involves putting the details of three holidays into the brochures for 18–30 year olds and 50+ year olds, respectively.

To help you decide which holidays go in which brochures you have information on a number of existing packages.

For 18–30 year olds:

Extreme Adventures: A collection of adventure holidays in exotic locations. Customers need to be physically fit and enjoy a challenge. These are holidays for the individualist and prices start in the medium range.

Sun Worshippers: Holidays for those who want to soak up the sun. Based mainly in Mediterranean resorts, these packages represent good value for money, with many priced in the economy range. Special deals are available for groups of friends wishing to holiday together.

After Dark: All-action weekend breaks in the major European capitals. Ideal for those who like music, dancing and partying the night away. These are breaks for people who want to have fun! Prices start in the economy range.

For 50+ year olds:

Golden Cruises: Sophisticated luxury cruises to islands in the West Indies. Customers need to enjoy group excursions, although there are opportunities for individual activities. All cruise prices fall in the expensive price range.

Great Cities: Two- or three-day breaks in famous European cities. The package includes accompanied tours of major museums, art galleries and sites of architectural interest. Prices fall in the economy and medium price ranges.

Craft Breaks: Ideal for people who want to learn a new craft such as pottery or weaving, these holidays include accommodation, travel, food and expert tuition. All are based in the UK and most are priced in the economy range.

Task

Which holiday goes in which brochure? In each case the answer is 18–30, 50+ or 'Cannot Tell'.

1. *Condor Trek*. A week-long break in South America exploring ancient jungle ruins. The highlight is a hang-gliding adventure from the top of the highest ziggurat. Not for the faint hearted! The price falls in the expensive range.

2. *Berlin Beer Festival*. A long weekend at the most famous beer festival of them all. Ideal for singles and groups, there is time to explore the cultural side of the city and to sample the beers to the early hours. The price falls in the economy range.

3. *Polar Adventure*. A unique opportunity to travel beyond the Artic Circle and experience the Polar Region. This cruising holiday is hosted aboard the luxurious *SS North Star* and the price falls in the expensive range.

Given the information you have on the different holiday packages the answer to question (1) is 18–30, question (2) is 'Cannot Tell' and question (3) is 50+.

The other two main developments in ability testing concern the move to more novel formats, and so-called Cognitive Process Profiling. A good example of the first is *Fastrack* from Saville & Holdsworth Ltd. This is a test for high-ability graduate and management candidates that is designed to assess problem-solving and analysis. It helps an employer decide how well a person is likely to apply his reasoning and judgement when making decisions, particularly when he is faced with new information.

The candidate is given information on a variety of different situations. This is presented on a number of cards that reflect the way in which we naturally receive information – from a range of different sources. The candidate then has to sort through the material, identify what is important, link together the different pieces of information, and use what has been discovered to solve problems.

In some ways, *Fastrack* is similar to the ABLE tests described previously, as both are trying to simulate aspects of business decision making and learning.

Cognitive Process Profiling

Cognitive Process Profiling is designed to look at your cognitive style (how you think), learning potential, strengths and limitations, and most appropriate working environment. This is a brand new technique and the best current example is the *Cognitive Process Profile* from ASE.

The Cognitive Process Profile is a computer simulation exercise that measures a person on 10,000 'mouse-click' points. It is a self-administered assessment in the form of a simulated card game that takes about two hours to complete.

As a selection tool, it provides information on how consistently a person approaches new and difficult problems, and their cognitive style. Are they analytic, structured, impulsive, random, or do they show the characteristics of any one of 16 different styles? Intriguingly, the assessment also provides a guide to someone's ideal work situation. The situations or 'environments' are:

- **Operational:** dealing with concrete, well defined tasks one by one. For example, clerical or production work.
- **Diagnostic:** accumulating information and using this to understand and overcome anticipated problems. For example, sales or educational work.

- **Alternative:** dealing with a whole operating system, optimizing all the available resources. For example, legal or medical work, senior management.
- **Parallel processing:** co-ordinating interacting programmes of activity, operating in parallel. For example, general managers or professional partners.
- **Strategic:** 'big systems' thinking, creating new structures and dealing with large-scale change. For example, CEOs of large organizations.

The key point about Cognitive Process Profiling is that the concern is not necessarily over getting the 'right' answers, but in describing the route a person uses to reach an answer. The profile approach also measures improvements in problem-solving from one item to another, and so provides an index of learning potential.

Virtual reality (VR)

Other developments include the use of VR to put you 'inside' a test. Thus, by wearing the appropriate equipment it will be possible to place you in a world of tests in which you can 'see' and 'feel' the questions. This may sound like science fiction but a number of systems do already exist, and VR-based exercises are already used for selection and training by the US Airforce and the British Royal Navy.

The pace of technological change is such that within the next 10 to 20 years it is reasonable to suppose that a combination of new test designs, VR and the world wide web will allow any person anywhere in the world to be assessed using a realistic simulation of any job.

Computer gaming systems also give us a clue as to how things may develop. It is only necessary to think about innovations such as Nintendo® Wii. This has a wireless controller that can be used as a pointing device, which can also detect motion in three dimensions. Clearly this technology could easily be used to develop a new range of spatial ability or manual dexterity tests.

Ten more ways to improve your performance

The details and hints given for each type of ability test will help you to prepare for most forms of testing. The key points listed at the end of Chapter 2 also provide important guidance on how to prepare for a test session. However, as you will see, there are a number of additional tips that can also help.

Tip 1: keep going!

As I have suggested elsewhere, the best policy is to try and complete as many questions as you can in the time allowed. However, you will find that different tests have different time limits. For example, here are the timing ranges for the tests covered in this chapter:

- Abstract Reasoning   30–40 minutes
- Verbal Reasoning   15–20 minutes
- Verbal Critical Reasoning   30–40 minutes
- Numerical Reasoning   15–20 minutes
- Numerical Critical Reasoning   30–40 minutes
- Perceptual Reasoning   15–20 minutes
- Spatial Reasoning   10–20 minutes
- Mechanical Reasoning   15–20 minutes
- Data Checking   8–10 minutes
- Manual Dexterity   5–8 minutes

Clearly, while it's good advice not to waste time on questions that you find difficult, you have more scope in some tests than in others to go back to a question you have not answered. As a rule of thumb, if a test is under about 10 minutes long it's better just to answer as many questions as you can, and not to return to those you may have left out.

Tip 2: double-check your answers

It is often suggested that when you attempt to answer the questions in a test that your first impressions are usually correct. This implies that if you have the time it is better to try and answer any questions you have left out, rather than change any of your existing answers. Interestingly, research has shown this to be an incorrect assumption, with one US study indicating that you may be three times as likely to change a wrong answer to a right one, than to make a right answer wrong. This suggests that any time you spend double-checking is time well spent.

Tip 3: guess with intelligence

If you do not know the answer to a question, should you guess? The two things to consider are how you're going to guess, and whether or not the test is negatively scored. When tests are negatively scored you have marks deducted for incorrect answers. This may or may not be announced at the beginning of the test, but if the instructions say that you should not guess then it is actually better to leave questions out. Conversely, if the instructions suggest that you should not leave any questions out, then it is probably safe to guess.

On the subject of how to guess, it is better to guess the answers to questions about which you have some knowledge. For example, if there are five options and you can completely eliminate two of them, you have a one-third chance of hitting the right answer. These are obviously better odds than a pure guess, which would give you a one-in-five chance of picking the correct response. However, you should bear in mind that if you are forced to guess a lot of the answers, even if you can reduce each to a one-in-three chance, then you are unlikely to score a very high mark. The reason is that your chance of correctly guessing the first question is one-in-three, and of the second question is one-in-three, but of correctly guessing both of them your chance is one-in-nine (one-third *times* one-third).

The more you guess, the worse are the overall odds. Even so, informed guesswork is much better than randomly picking the answers.

Tip 4: read the questions twice

Many people work out the correct answer to a problem and then fill in the answer sheet incorrectly. A common mistake is to mix up the answer choices. Consider the following example:

Example 23: Verbal Sequences
What is the next word but one in the following sequence?
Century...   Decade...   Year...   Month...?
(a) Hour   (b) Minute   (c) Day   (d) Week   (e) Second

It's easy to look at a question like that and to decide correctly that (c) is the right answer, but to mark (d) instead. That's because you have confused 'd' with the first letter of 'day'. Another thing that people do is misread the question. In this case not to notice that the question asks for *the next word but one*. This would mean that while you fully understood the sequence you would answer (d) again, which of course is incorrect. The moral of the story is always to pay very close attention to the questions, otherwise you will lose marks even when you actually know the correct answers.

Tip 5: estimate your answers

In most numerical tests the questions are usually designed so that you do not have to work out the answers exactly in order to choose the correct responses. This would imply that it is better to work out rough answers and check them against the options rather than spend time calculating things precisely.

Tip 6: don't be afraid of numbers

An ability to deal with numbers is a key requirement in many jobs. If you don't like mathematics the *only* way you are going to improve is to face your fear head on. Go to a library or a bookshop, find a maths book you understand, and work through some examples.

Tip 7: watch out for distractors

When test questions are written the designer will include different types of answer choices. Naturally, one of these will be the correct answer, but the others will be distinct sorts of incorrect answers. Here are some examples:

- If the correct answer is '67.5' a number of 'distractors' will be included such as '6.75', 675 and 6750. The estimation approach suggested in Tip 5 should help you to avoid picking any of these by accident.
- Body is to food as engine is to: (a) spark (b) wheels (c) fuel (d) exhaust.
  The correct answer is (c), but it's surrounded by distractors, all of which are related to the word 'engine'.

The trick with distractors is to realize that they are there in the first place, and not to be seduced by things like near misses, or word associations.

Tip 8: think about the question order

It makes sense to answer the questions you find the easiest first. This means that it is not always advisable to answer the questions in the order presented. However, if you do adopt this tactic, make sure you do not get out of sequence on the answer sheet. Also, if you read the questions as you go along you will find that your unconscious mind has a chance to work on them, and sometimes you will find it much easier to get the answer when you return for a second time.

Tip 9: use all your time allowance

Even if you are finding a test hard going, use all the time you are allowed, and work right up to the last second. If you finish early double- and triple-check your answers.

Tip 10: practise, practise, practise!

Sometimes a few more marks will make all the difference. It pays to put as much energy as you can into preparing yourself for psychometric tests.

Key points

- There are about 50 different abilities that can be measured, but most assessments are based on combinations of only 6 types of test.
- The most frequently used tests measure abstract, verbal, numerical, perceptual, spatial and mechanical reasoning.
- Other types of test measure psychomotor abilities like hand–eye co-ordination; physical abilities like static strength (the ability to use continuous muscle force to lift, push and carry – important in jobs like firefighting); and sensory abilities, such as correct colour vision (important for designers, electricians, chemists and pilots).
- Each type of ability test has characteristic types of questions. Extensive details have been given in this chapter.
- There are exercises you can do to prepare for any test that is based on knowledge or experience (attainment tests). You can also improve your performance on other types of tests by following the hints provided.

- Preparation is the key to test success. No employer will expect you to be an authority on tests, or test taking, but intelligent preparation in the weeks before a test session will help to give you an edge over the other candidates.
- In those cases where employers use cut-off scores (see Chapter 1), a few extra marks can make the difference between success and failure. Ensure that you do not make avoidable mistakes.
- There are many sources of valuable information and practice material, such as textbooks, quiz books and books containing example questions. These can all be bought in large bookshops, or are available from libraries.

4

Practice tests (technical, clerical and graduate)

Introduction to SHL® practice tests

This chapter contains three sets of practice tests. These have been supplied by Saville & Holdsworth Ltd and are the type of practice tests you will encounter before a real session. Tests like these are used in selection and assessment, as well as in careers guidance and development.

Each test comes with a set of instructions and a guide to the time you should spend answering the questions. It is important to stick to the suggested times, as this will give you an idea of the pace required for full-length tests of this type.

Series 1 contains six different tests. These are Working with Words, Working with Numbers, Working with Diagrams, Checking Information, Recognizing Shapes and Mechanical Understanding. The first four are basic-level assessments, the shapes and mechanical tests are applicable to all levels of ability.

Series 2 presents three rather harder tests concerned with Interpreting Written Information, Interpreting Data and

Interpreting Diagrams. These would be used with candidates who had a good basic level of education.

Series 3 contains the hardest tests and focuses on Verbal Reasoning, Numerical Reasoning and Diagrammatic Reasoning. Tests of this sort are aimed at those with a good post-16 education. The format is also quite typical of graduate-level tests.

The best way to use these practice questions is to start with those that you think are the correct level. When you have completed the appropriate series move on to the others and see how they feel in comparison. The answers are provided at the back of the book.

Series 1

Test 1: working with words

This test looks at your ability to understand written instructions. Use the information given in the passage to answer the questions that follow. For each question, you have to select the correct answer from the five choices given, and fill in the appropriate circle.

Time guideline: See how many questions you can answer in 3 minutes.

Start when you are ready.

Local drama group

Are you interested in acting? If you are, please come to a meeting about the Amateur Dramatics Society's next play. You don't need any experience of acting – so give it a try! The meeting will take place in the local Community Centre on 10th June between 3 and 5 pm.

We also need about 20 musicians to play music during the play. Musicians do not need to attend the meeting, but should contact Ms Patel at the Community Centre before the 17th June to arrange an audition.

People who are interested in decorating the stage set or providing technical assistance should contact the Amateur Dramatics Society direct.

Rehearsals will take place every Tuesday evening. Performances are planned for the 18th and 30th of August.

1. Who should attend the meeting on the 10th June?
   A   Anyone with an interest in acting.
   B   About 20 musicians.
   C   Only people with experience of acting.
   D   Only people without experience of acting.
   E   All members of the Amateur Dramatics Society.

2. When will the rehearsals take place?
   A   17th June.
   B   Every Tuesday evening.
   C   18th and 30th August.
   D   10th June.
   E   None of these.

3. What should any musicians do?
   A   Make sure they go to the meeting on the 10th June.
   B   Wait for Ms Patel to contact them.
   C   Contact the Amateur Dramatics Society.
   D   Ring Ms Patel at home.
   E   None of these.

Vending machine – operating instructions

To obtain a drink follow these instructions:

- Remove plastic cup from dispenser and place directly under spout for drink required.
- Insert exact coins or tokens available from Reception.
- Press selected button once and wait until spout has completed pouring before lifting safety cover and removing cup.
- Sugar and milk powder can be dispensed without charge by placing cup under appropriate spout and pressing button once or twice as required.

Any faults in operation of machine should be reported immediately to the Maintenance Supervisor. Refunds can then be obtained from Reception.

4. What is the first stage in obtaining a drink?
    A   Insert the exact coins.
    B   Press the selected button.
    C   Take a plastic cup from dispenser.
    D   Insert the token and press the selected button.
    E   Obtain a plastic cup from Reception.

5. What is available free of charge?
    A   Only drinks.
    B   Only sugar and milk powder.
    C   Only plastic cups.
    D   Only drinks, sugar and milk powder.
    E   Only sugar, milk powder and plastic cups.

6. How can you obtain a refund?
    A   By contacting the Maintenance Supervisor.
    B   By pressing the 'refund' button.
    C   By inserting another token.
    D   From Reception (after reporting the fault).
    E   None of these.

Answer sheet 1

1. Ⓐ Ⓑ Ⓒ Ⓓ Ⓔ
2. Ⓐ Ⓑ Ⓒ Ⓓ Ⓔ
3. Ⓐ Ⓑ Ⓒ Ⓓ Ⓔ
4. Ⓐ Ⓑ Ⓒ Ⓓ Ⓔ
5. Ⓐ Ⓑ Ⓒ Ⓓ Ⓔ
6. Ⓐ Ⓑ Ⓒ Ⓓ Ⓔ

Test 2: working with numbers

This test looks at your ability to make quick and accurate calculations. Identify the number which should replace the '?' in each question, and fill in the appropriate circle.

Time guideline: See how many questions you can answer in **3 minutes,** without using a calculator.

Start when you are ready.

	A	B	C	D	E

1. | 9 | – | ? | = | 4 |

| 2 | 3 | 4 | 5 | 13 |

2. | 14 | × | 3 | = | ? |

| 11 | 17 | 42 | 56 | 143 |

3. | 20% | of | ? | = | 10 |

| 2 | 10 | 20 | 50 | 100 |

4. | 16 | ÷ | 2 | = | ? | – | 4 |

| 4 | 6 | 8 | 10 | 12 |

5. | ½ | – | ? | = | ¼ |

| ⅛ | ¼ | ½ | 1 | 8 |

6. | 15.3 | ÷ | 5.1 | = | ? |

| 1 | 2 | 3 | 4 | 5 |

7. | ? | + | 50 | = | 10 | × | 12 |

| 60 | 70 | 80 | 90 | 100 |

8. | 25% | of | 12.44 | = | ? |

| 3.11 | 6.22 | 12.44 | 311 | 622 |

Answer sheet 2

1. Ⓐ Ⓑ Ⓒ Ⓓ Ⓔ
2. Ⓐ Ⓑ Ⓒ Ⓓ Ⓔ
3. Ⓐ Ⓑ Ⓒ Ⓓ Ⓔ
4. Ⓐ Ⓑ Ⓒ Ⓓ Ⓔ
5. Ⓐ Ⓑ Ⓒ Ⓓ Ⓔ
6. Ⓐ Ⓑ Ⓒ Ⓓ Ⓔ
7. Ⓐ Ⓑ Ⓒ Ⓓ Ⓔ
8. Ⓐ Ⓑ Ⓒ Ⓓ Ⓔ

Test 3: working with diagrams

This test looks at your ability to follow instructions coded as symbols.

In this test columns of shapes are presented in BOXES. You have to change these shapes using commands that are shown as symbols contained in CIRCLES.

A complete list of these commands and what they do is given below.

Work down the column starting at the top, and change the shapes according to the command symbols given.

Select the answer that would result from applying the commands, and fill in the appropriate circle.

Time guidelines: See how many questions you can answer in **3 minutes.**

Commands

(∩)   Turn the shape upside down

(⌀)   Remove the contents of this box

(�G)   Swap the shape in this box with the shape in the box below

(✶)   Cancel the previous command

(↕)   Present all shapes in the column in REVERSE order

Start when you are ready.

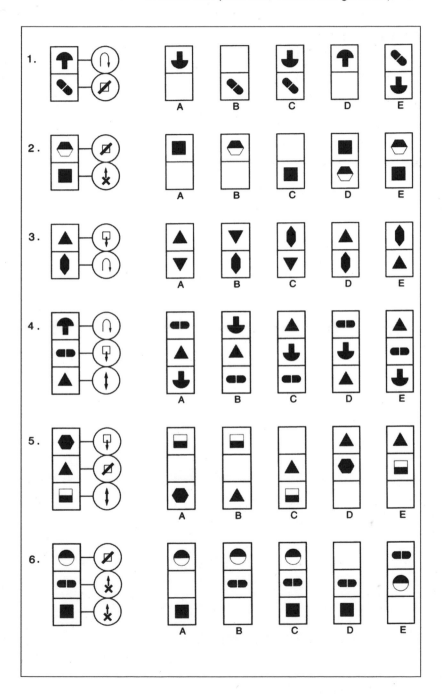

Answer sheet 3

1. (A) (B) (C) (D) (E)
2. (A) (B) (C) (D) (E)
3. (A) (B) (C) (D) (E)
4. (A) (B) (C) (D) (E)
5. (A) (B) (C) (D) (E)
6. (A) (B) (C) (D) (E)

Test 4: checking information

This test looks at your ability to check information quickly and accurately. You are given two lists of reference numbers, the original handwritten list on the left, and the final typed list on the right. You have to look for any differences (errors) between the two lists. Fill in the circle for any column where you find a difference. If there are no differences (errors) in a line, fill in circle E. Remember there can be more than one error in the line, so you may have to fill in more than one circle for a question.

Time guideline: See how many questions you can answer in **2 minutes.**

Start when you are ready.

	A	B	C	D	A	B	C	D
1.	12	KT	3D	47–98	22	KT	3D	47–98
2.	91	PM	C5	62–64	91	PM	C5	62–64
3.	3	AJ	B4	L55–57	3	JA	B4	L51–55
4.	17	AM	S5	B7–22	18	PM	S5	B7–12
5.	11	ZZ	PO	M9–10	11	ZZ	PO	M9–10
6.	89	SR	X8	F14–16	98	XR	Y9	F14–16
7.	34	XX	K7	35–38	34	YY	K7	35–39
8.	87	KP	M6	A12–13	87	M6	KP	A12–13
9.	7	JZ	K2	H8–9	7	JZ	K2	H8–9
10.	69	JI	S5	K66–69	96	IJ	5S	K64–66

Answer sheet 4

1. Ⓐ Ⓑ Ⓒ Ⓓ Ⓔ
2. Ⓐ Ⓑ Ⓒ Ⓓ Ⓔ
3. Ⓐ Ⓑ Ⓒ Ⓓ Ⓔ
4. Ⓐ Ⓑ Ⓒ Ⓓ Ⓔ
5. Ⓐ Ⓑ Ⓒ Ⓓ Ⓔ
6. Ⓐ Ⓑ Ⓒ Ⓓ Ⓔ
7. Ⓐ Ⓑ Ⓒ Ⓓ Ⓔ
8. Ⓐ Ⓑ Ⓒ Ⓓ Ⓔ
9. Ⓐ Ⓑ Ⓒ Ⓓ Ⓔ
10. Ⓐ Ⓑ Ⓒ Ⓓ Ⓔ

Test 5: recognizing shapes

This test looks at your ability to recognize identical shapes. Study the shape on the left, and after viewing all the choices, decide which of the shapes on the right is the same. Note that while the shapes may be turned around on the page, they are not flipped over.

Time guideline: See how many questions you can answer in **2 minutes**.

Start when you are ready.

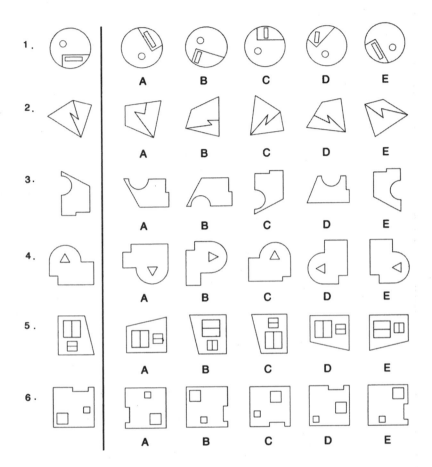

Answer sheet 5

1. Ⓐ Ⓑ Ⓒ Ⓓ Ⓔ
2. Ⓐ Ⓑ Ⓒ Ⓓ Ⓔ
3. Ⓐ Ⓑ Ⓒ Ⓓ Ⓔ
4. Ⓐ Ⓑ Ⓒ Ⓓ Ⓔ
5. Ⓐ Ⓑ Ⓒ Ⓓ Ⓔ
6. Ⓐ Ⓑ Ⓒ Ⓓ Ⓔ

Test 6: mechanical understanding

This test looks at your ability to understand mechanical principles and practical problems. Each problem consists of a question that refers to a drawing. Look at each drawing and answer the question that follows, filling in the appropriate circle on the Answer Sheet panel.

Time guidelines: See how many questions you can answer in **2 minutes.**

Start when you are ready.

1. Which spanner makes it easier to undo the nut?

   If equal, mark C.

2. Which shelf should support the heaviest load?

3. How many pulleys turn clockwise?

A	B	C
1	2	3

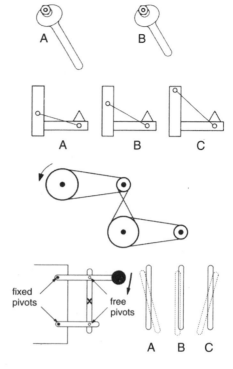

4. How will link 'X' move when the handle is operated as shown?

Answer sheet 6

1. Ⓐ Ⓑ Ⓒ
2. Ⓐ Ⓑ Ⓒ
3. Ⓐ Ⓑ Ⓒ
4. Ⓐ Ⓑ Ⓒ

Series 2

Test 1: interpreting written information

This test looks at your ability to understand written passages and evaluate the logic of written argument. The test consists of a series of passages, each of which is followed by several statements. Your task is to evaluate each statement in the light of the passage and to mark the appropriate circle, following the rules given below.

Mark Circle A
if the statement is **TRUE**, given the information or opinions contained in the passage.

Mark Circle B
if the statement is **FALSE**, given the information or opinions contained in the passage.

Mark Circle C
if you **CANNOT SAY** whether the statement is true or false without further information.

The test assesses your ability to reason with written information. It is not a test of your general knowledge and you should only base your answers on the information contained in the passage.

Time guideline: See how many questions you can answer in 5 **minutes.**

Start when you are ready.

Many organizations find it beneficial to employ students during the summer. Permanent staff often wish to take their own holidays over this period. Furthermore, it is not uncommon for companies to experience peak workloads in the summer and so require extra staff. Summer employment also attracts students who may return as well-qualified recruits to an organization when they have completed their education. Ensuring that the students learn as much as possible about the organization encourages their interest in working on a permanent basis. Organizations pay students on a fixed rate without the usual entitlement to paid holiday or sick leave.

1. It is possible that permanent staff who are on holiday can have their work carried out by students.

2. Students in summer employment are given the same paid holiday benefits as permanent staff.

3. Students are subject to the organization's standard disciplinary and grievance procedures.

4. Some companies have more work to do in the summer when students are available for vacation work.

Most banks and building societies adopt a 'no smoking' policy in customer areas in their branches. Plaques and stickers are displayed in these areas to draw customers' attention to this policy. These notices are worded in a 'customer friendly' manner, although a few customers may feel their personal freedom of choice is being infringed. If a customer does ignore a notice, staff are tolerant and avoid making a great issue of the situation. In fact, the majority of customers now expect such a 'no smoking' policy in premises of this kind. After all, such a policy improves the pleasantness of the customer facilities and also lessens fire risk.

5. 'No smoking' policies have mainly been introduced in response to customer demand.

6. All banks and building societies now have a 'no smoking' policy.

7. There is no conflict of interest between a 'no smoking' policy and personal freedom of choice for all.

8. A 'no smoking' policy is in line with most customers' expectations in banks and building societies.

Answer sheet 1

1. Ⓐ Ⓑ Ⓒ
2. Ⓐ Ⓑ Ⓒ
3. Ⓐ Ⓑ Ⓒ
4. Ⓐ Ⓑ Ⓒ
5. Ⓐ Ⓑ Ⓒ
6. Ⓐ Ⓑ Ⓒ
7. Ⓐ Ⓑ Ⓒ
8. Ⓐ Ⓑ Ⓒ

Test 2: interpreting data

This test looks at your ability to understand graphs and statistical tables and to draw appropriate conclusions from them. You will be using facts and figures presented in various ways to answer a range of questions. In each question you are given five answers to choose from. One and only one of the answers is correct in each case.

Time guideline: See how many questions you can answer in **5 minutes.**

Start when you are ready.

MACHINE PRODUCTION

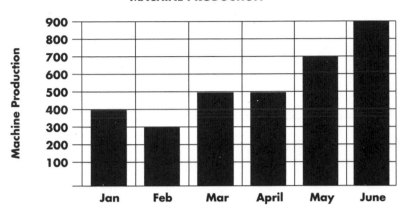

1. How many machines were produced in the first three months of the period?

A	B	C	D	E
900	1000	1100	1200	None of these

2. If the trend of the last 3 months continues, how many machines will be produced in July?

A	B	C	D	E
1100	1200	1300	1400	Cannot say

3. In which month did machine production figures show the greatest percentage change, relative to the previous month?

A	B	C	D	E
February	March	April	May	June

4. What was the combined readership of *Home Hints*, *Travel Plus* and *Leisure Time* in 1983 (in millions)? (See page 108.)

A	B	C	D	E
7.2	16.5	20.8	37.3	None of these

5. What percentage of copies of *Computer News* were sold in specialist computer shops in 1993?

A	B	C	D	E
24%	34%	42%	66%	Cannot say

MAGAZINE READERSHIP

Magazine Title	Estimated No of Readers (millions)		Percentage of copies sold in 1993, by outlet:	
	1983	1993	Subscription	Newsagents
Home Hints	4.8	2.4	47%	13%
Business Tomorrow	1.1	1.4	58%	24%
Computer News	2.3	4.6	34%	24%
Travel Plus	8.5	6.1	25%	44%
Leisure Time	7.5	8.0	28%	47%

6. If 1.0 million copies of *Travel Plus* were sold by subscription, how many copies were sold overall in 1993 (in millions)?

A	B	C	D	E
1	2.9	4	6.1	8.5

Answer sheet 2

1. Ⓐ Ⓑ Ⓒ Ⓓ Ⓔ
2. Ⓐ Ⓑ Ⓒ Ⓓ Ⓔ
3. Ⓐ Ⓑ Ⓒ Ⓓ Ⓔ
4. Ⓐ Ⓑ Ⓒ Ⓓ Ⓔ
5. Ⓐ Ⓑ Ⓒ Ⓓ Ⓔ
6. Ⓐ Ⓑ Ⓒ Ⓓ Ⓔ

Test 3: interpreting diagrams

This test looks at your ability to recognize rules within logical sequences, and to apply them to given problems. You are shown a number of diagrams in which figures in **boxes** are altered by commands (letters) in **circles**.

The commands alter a figure by changing its size, colour or shape in general or specific ways.

Paths through each diagram are identified by black or white arrows. You must follow paths that only include one type of arrow.

In this test, you have to work out what each command does and then answer the questions immediately below each diagram.

Now look at the first diagram.

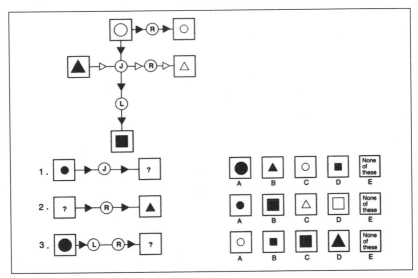

In the first diagram, it can be seen that command **R** reduces the size of the figure in the box; it changes a large circle into a small circle.

Following the white arrows across, we can see that **J** and **R** together, reduce the size of the figure and change its colour, here from black to white.

Since we know that **R** reduces the size of the figure, we can now say that **J** changes its colour.

Working down, **J** and **L** together change the colour, this time from white to black, and also the shape of the figure, from a circle to a square. Having established that **J** changes colour, we can now say that **L** changes the shape of a figure.

Now applying these commands to the first question, we have seen that **J** changes the colour of the figure, therefore producing a small white circle, answer C.

In question 2, **R** reduces the size of a figure, so we can say that what is missing is a large black triangle, answer E.

In question 3, **L** changes the circle into a square, and **R** reduces its size, so the result is a small black square, answer B.

Now, make sure that you understand these answers and then go on and do the next set of questions, 4 to 6, by yourself.

Time guideline: See if you can do Questions 4 to 6 in **3 minutes.**

Start when you are ready.

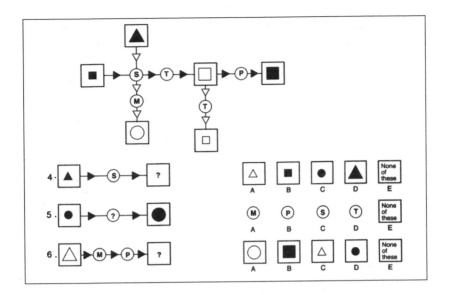

Answer sheet 3

1. Ⓐ Ⓑ Ⓒ Ⓓ Ⓔ
2. Ⓐ Ⓑ Ⓒ Ⓓ Ⓔ
3. Ⓐ Ⓑ Ⓒ Ⓓ Ⓔ
4. Ⓐ Ⓑ Ⓒ Ⓓ Ⓔ
5. Ⓐ Ⓑ Ⓒ Ⓓ Ⓔ
6. Ⓐ Ⓑ Ⓒ Ⓓ Ⓔ

Series 3

Test 1: verbal reasoning

This test looks at your ability to understand and reason with written information. The test consists of a series of passages, each of which is followed by several statements. Your task is to evaluate each statement in the light of the passage which precedes it and to mark the appropriate circle, following the rules given below.

Mark Circle A
if the statement is **TRUE** or follows logically, given the information or opinions contained in the passage.

Mark Circle B
if the statement is **FALSE** or the opposite follows logically, given the information or opinions contained in the passage.

Mark Circle C
if you **CANNOT SAY** whether the statement is true or false without further information.

This test is not a test of your general knowledge and you should only base your answers on the information contained in the passage.

Time guideline: See how many questions you can answer in **5 minutes**.

Start when you are ready.

A principal objective of the Health and Safety at Work Act 1974 is to involve everybody in the workplace. The promotion of health and safety is an essential function of good management in all areas. The employer, however, also has a duty to protect other persons on the premises. The term 'premises' includes all workplaces, and in particular, includes any vehicle, vessel, aircraft, or any other installation on land. Regulations may be made exempting certain employers from the necessity to provide all employees with written copies of the Act.

1. The Health and Safety Act is the sole responsibility of the employee.

2. All installations on land, and vehicles are subsumed under the heading 'premises'.

3. The Act states that all employees must receive written copies.

4. There were no health and safety rules before 1974.

The government has attempted to integrate the environmental clean-up of industry under one umbrella. To minimize environmental damage, the volume of pollutants emitted from a plant has to be authorized by an official pollution control inspectorate. Industry has complained repeatedly about the time and cost of getting operations approved under the new system. The inspectors maintain, however, that industry often has itself to blame for delays, as many applications provide insufficient data. Industry has also worried about public access to the information it supplies to get authorization. Information can only be withheld from public registers on the grounds of commercial confidentiality, if a company can prove it would be disadvantaged by disclosure.

5. The new pollution control system was set up to reduce the number of toxins used by industry.

6. Obtaining authorization on operations results in having to divulge confidential information to competitors.

7. Industry has not welcomed the introduction of the official pollution control inspectorate.

8. There would be no environmental destruction if there were no pollutants.

Answer sheet 1

1. Ⓐ Ⓑ Ⓒ
2. Ⓐ Ⓑ Ⓒ
3. Ⓐ Ⓑ Ⓒ
4. Ⓐ Ⓑ Ⓒ
5. Ⓐ Ⓑ Ⓒ
6. Ⓐ Ⓑ Ⓒ
7. Ⓐ Ⓑ Ⓒ
8. Ⓐ Ⓑ Ⓒ

Test 2: numerical reasoning

This test looks at your ability to understand facts and figures presented in various ways and to draw appropriate conclusions from them. You should base your answers only on the information contained in the tables and graphs and not on any prior knowledge. In each question you are given five answers to choose from. One and only one of the answers is correct in each case. You can use a calculator to help you.

Time guideline: See how many questions you can answer in **5 minutes.**

Start when you are ready.

NEWSPAPER READERSHIP

Daily Newspapers	Readership (millions)		Percentage of copies sold in Year 2, by outlet:	
	Year 1	Year 2	Subscription	Newsagents
The Daily Chronicle	3.6	2.9	47%	37%
The Daily News	14.8	10.0	50%	33%
The Tribune	1.1	1.4	43%	43%
The Herald	8.4	10.9	29%	55%
The Daily Echo	4.8	4.9	30%	60%

1. What was the combined readership of *The Daily Chronicle*, *The Tribune* and *The Daily Echo* in Year 2 (in millions)?

A	B	C	D	E
9.2	9.5	18.7	31.8	None of these

2. Which Daily Newspaper showed the largest percentage change in readership from Year 1 to Year 2?

A	B	C	D	E
The Daily Chronicle	The Daily News	The Tribune	The Herald	The Daily Echo

3. If 4.5 million copies of *The Daily News* were sold by Subscription, approximately how many copies (in millions) were sold by Newsagents in Year 2?

A	B	C	D	E
1.5	2.3	3	6	Cannot say

4. What was the selling price for Mountain Bikes if the sales income for this product was £140,000 in January? (See chart overleaf.)

A	B	C	D	E
300	350	400	450	500

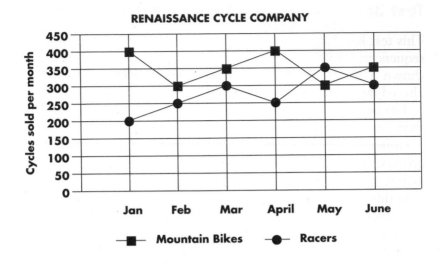

RENAISSANCE CYCLE COMPANY

5. What was the percentage increase in the selling price of Racers between January and June?

A	B	C	D	E
0%	10%	20%	50%	Cannot say

6. If Racers sell for twice as much as Mountain Bikes, in which month was the total sales income highest?

A	B	C	D	E
February	March	April	May	June

Answer sheet 2

1. Ⓐ Ⓑ Ⓒ Ⓓ Ⓔ
2. Ⓐ Ⓑ Ⓒ Ⓓ Ⓔ
3. Ⓐ Ⓑ Ⓒ Ⓓ Ⓔ
4. Ⓐ Ⓑ Ⓒ Ⓓ Ⓔ
5. Ⓐ Ⓑ Ⓒ Ⓓ Ⓔ
6. Ⓐ Ⓑ Ⓒ Ⓓ Ⓔ

Test 3: diagrammatic reasoning

This test looks at your ability to recognize rules within logical sequences, and to apply them to given problems. You are shown a number of diagrams in which figures in **boxes** are altered by commands (symbols) in **circles**.

The commands alter a figure by changing its size, colour or shape in general or specific ways.

Paths through each diagram are identified by black or white arrows. You must follow paths that only include one type of arrow.

In this test, you have to work out what each command does and then answer the questions immediately below each diagram.

Now look at the first diagram.

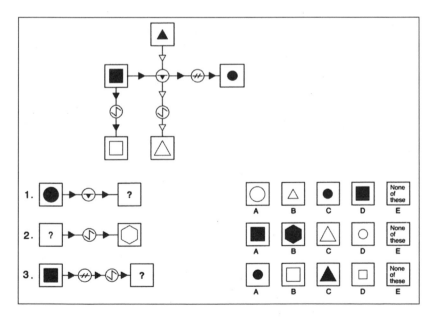

Working down from the black square in the first diagram, it can be seen that command ⊘ changes a black square into a white square.

Following the white arrows down, we can see that the two commands ⊙ and ⊕ together, increase the size of a triangle, and **also** change its colour from black to white.

We already know that ⊕ changes the colour of the figure; therefore ⊙ must change its size, here from small to large.

Working across, ⊙ and ⊛ together **reduce** the size of the figure and also change its shape, from a square to a circle. We can now say that ⊙ **reverses** the size of the figure, therefore ⊛ changes its shape.

Now applying these commands to the first question, we have seen that ⊙ reverses the size of the figure therefore producing a small black circle, answer C.

In question 2, ⊕ changes the colour of a figure from black to white, so we can say that the missing figure is a large black hexagon, answer B.

In question 3, ⊛ changes the square into a circle, and ⊕ changes its colour from black to white. The result is a large white circle, answer E.

Time guideline: See if you do Questions 4 to 6 in **3 minutes**. Start when you are ready.

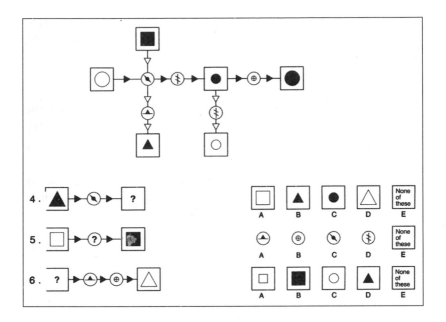

Answer sheet 3

1. Ⓐ Ⓑ Ⓒ Ⓓ Ⓔ
2. Ⓐ Ⓑ Ⓒ Ⓓ Ⓔ
3. Ⓐ Ⓑ Ⓒ Ⓓ Ⓔ
4. Ⓐ Ⓑ Ⓒ Ⓓ Ⓔ
5. Ⓐ Ⓑ Ⓒ Ⓓ Ⓔ
6. Ⓐ Ⓑ Ⓒ Ⓓ Ⓔ

Practice tests (graduate and university admissions)

Introduction to Team Focus practice tests

Team Focus Ltd are a firm of occupational psychologists that specialize in the development of online assessment tests and questionnaires. Over the last few years they have designed an impressive range of ability and personality tests and other measures that are all available via the internet. These tests and questionnaires are used by employers and universities for selection and development purposes. For example, it is useful to know how your thinking skills compare with those of other job applicants or potential students, or to explore learning style and career preferences.

Each of the online tests and questionnaires on offer takes about 15 minutes to complete, and results are returned instantly by e-mail. The following section includes some genuine practice material from Team Focus for you to try, with the answers provided at the end of the book. The tests look at abstract, verbal and numerical reasoning.

It is rare for test publishers to offer 'open' access to a range of full-length, professionally developed tests and question-naires. If you would like to complete the actual tests and ques-tionnaires, they can be accessed easily at **www.profilingfor success.com**; or if you are interested in university entrance tests, at **www.drtest.co.uk.** You can complete a single test or questionnaire, or a combination.

It is also possible to complete a 'taster' assessment that has been devised to go with this book. If you would like to try this free test, which includes a feedback report, go to **www.profilingforsuccess.com/kogan-page.**

Practice material

Test 1: abstract reasoning

The abstract reasoning items look at your ability to identify relationships between shapes. This ability is related to skills such as generating ideas and problem-solving.

For each set of items you will see two sets of shapes, labelled Set A and Set B. All of the shapes in Set A are similar in some way, as are the shapes in Set B. Set A and Set B are not related to each other.

You have to work out how the shapes in each set are related to each other. You then have to work out whether each of six further shapes belongs to Set A, Neither set, or Set B.

Time guideline: See how many questions you can do in **4 minutes.**

Start when you are ready.

1.

2.

3.

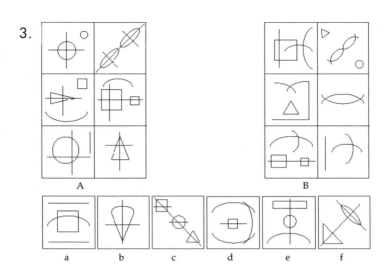

A   B

a   b   c   d   e   f

Answer sheet

	Mark the correct answer		
1a	Set A	Neither	Set B
1b	Set A	Neither	Set B
1c	Set A	Neither	Set B
1d	Set A	Neither	Set B
1e	Set A	Neither	Set B
1f	Set A	Neither	Set B
2a	Set A	Neither	Set B
2b	Set A	Neither	Set B
2c	Set A	Neither	Set B
2d	Set A	Neither	Set B
2e	Set A	Neither	Set B
2f	Set A	Neither	Set B
3a	Set A	Neither	Set B
3b	Set A	Neither	Set B
3c	Set A	Neither	Set B
3d	Set A	Neither	Set B
3e	Set A	Neither	Set B
3f	Set A	Neither	Set B

Test 2: verbal reasoning

The verbal reasoning items test your ability to think logically about written information. Below are passages of text, each followed by five statements. Your task is to read carefully each passage and then decide whether each statement follows logically from the information in the passage.

For each statement there are three options to choose from: True, False and Can't Tell.

- True – this means that, on the basis of the information in the passage, the statement is true or logically follows from the passage.
- False – this means that, on the basis of the information in the passage, the statement is false.
- Can't tell – this means that you cannot tell from the information in the passage whether the information is true or false.

When deciding whether a statement is true, false or you cannot tell, it is important to base your answer only on the information in the passage and not on any other knowledge you may have. Your task is simply to judge whether or not the statement follows logically from the passage.

Time guideline: See how many questions you can do in **4 minutes**.

Circle the correct answers and start when you are ready.

1. Want to find out more about flying? ... then join our cabin crew

You don't have to sign up for life – initially you start on a fixed-term contract, beginning with a comprehensive training programme which gives you a chance to see if this is really for you. To join us, you will need to demonstrate a high level of personal presentation, excellent communication skills and the ability to recognize, identify and respond to individual customer needs. Age doesn't matter – as long as you're over 20 and under 60 – but you must be fit, resilient and well-organized. So, if you enjoy using your initiative and welcome the chance to acquire new skills, this is the opportunity for you.

a) Before you join the airline, you must be sure that this is the right occupation for you.

b) This job requires some good 'people skills'.

c) The advert tells you how to apply to join the airline's cabin crew.

d) Age is not a factor in the airline's selection criteria.

e) The airline selects cabin crew at the end of the training programme.

2. Directions for taking cough medicine

Adults and children over 12 years: Two 5 ml spoonfuls four times a day.

Children 6–12 years: One 5 ml spoonful four times a day.

Children 2–5 years: One 5 ml spoonful twice a day.

X Not to be given to children under 2 years.

X Avoid alcoholic drink.

X Do not exceed the stated dose.

---

a) An adult should take 40 ml of the cough medicine per day.

b) Alcohol prevents the cough medicine from working.

c) A child of 7 can take the cough medicine as often as an adult.

d) If taken as directed, the cough medicine has no side effects.

e) Adults and children over 12 can take twice the daily amount of cough medicine as children aged 2–5 years.

3. Pennywise Bank has written the following letter to its customers:

I am writing to let you know that the interest we pay on your Super Savings account has been reduced. You will find the new rate in the enclosed leaflet. The leaflet gives the interest rates for all our investment accounts as well as the previous rates which applied.

As you know, we always write to tell you whenever we change the interest rate on your account because we are committed to the Banking Code. This voluntary code sets standards of good practice for banks and building societies in dealings with their personal customers. As well as writing to you, we will continue to use national newspapers to advertize rates on all our accounts, and we will display this information in your local branch.

a) Banks and building societies must abide by the Banking Code.

b) Pennywise Bank has reduced the interest rates on all its investment accounts.

c) The Banking Code does not apply to the bank's business customers.

d) You can find out how much interest Pennywise Bank charges on personal loans from the leaflet enclosed with this letter.

e) From the information leaflet, you could calculate the overall change in interest rate on your Super Savings account.

Answer sheet

	Mark the correct answer		
1a	True	False	Can't tell
1b	True	False	Can't tell
1c	True	False	Can't tell
1d	True	False	Can't tell
1e	True	False	Can't tell
2a	True	False	Can't tell
2b	True	False	Can't tell
2c	True	False	Can't tell
2d	True	False	Can't tell
2e	True	False	Can't tell
3a	True	False	Can't tell
3b	True	False	Can't tell
3c	True	False	Can't tell
3d	True	False	Can't tell
3e	True	False	Can't tell

Test 3: numerical reasoning

The numerical reasoning items look at your ability to solve numerical problems. For each set of items you will see some numerical information. Below this are five questions, each followed by five possible answer options, labelled 'a', 'b', 'c', 'd' and 'e'.

Work out the correct answer using the numerical information provided, then select one of the five options. Please note that you should not use a calculator for this test.

Time guideline: See how many you can do in **4 minutes**.

Circle the correct answers and start when you are ready.

1. The table below shows the annual cost of breakdown cover with two motoring organizations. The figures are given in pounds.

Type of cover	Motoring Organization	
	Blue Star	Green Arrow
Gold	75	90
Silver	65	60
Bronze	40	30

a) Next year, you intend to change from Blue Star Silver to Green Arrow Bronze cover. How much will you save?

   a) £5   b) £10   c) £25   d) £30   e) £35

b) Green Arrow offer 10% discount on the total cost of cover if you take out breakdown cover for more than one car. What is the cost of having two cars with Green Arrow Bronze cover?

   a) £46   b) £54   c) £60   d) £66   e) £72

c) Three members of a family share equally the cost of Silver cover for one car with Green Arrow. How much does each person pay?

   a) £20   b) £25   c) £30   d) £60   e) £180

d) What is the ratio of the cost of Silver cover with Green Arrow to Gold cover with Green Arrow?

   a) 1:3   b) 2:3   c) 3:2   d) 2:1   e) 3:1

e) If the cost of Blue Star Bronze cover increases to £50, what percentage increase is this?

   a) 10%   b) 20%   c) 25%   d) 50%   e) Can't tell

2. The letters p to u are used to represent coins as shown:

p	1p
q	2p
r	5p
s	10p
t	20p
u	50p

a) How much is p + q + r + t?

    a) 17p   b) 18p   c) 19p   d) 20p   e) 28p

b) How much is 5u + s?

    a) 35p   b) 65p   c) 100p   d) 260p   e) 300p

c) How much is (s + t)/5?

    a) 2p   b) 4p   c) 6p   d) 14p   e) 35p

d) What is the value of 2u/(r + t)?

    a) 2p   b) 4p   c) 5p   d) 20p   e) 40p

e) If z = p + q + r + s, which of the following is true?

    a) t = z   b) t > z and t − z > 5p   c) t > z and t − z < 5p
    d) t < z and t − z > 5p   e) t < z and t − z < 5p

3. Two surveys were conducted, asking people which political party they would vote for. The results are shown in the table below.

	Survey A	Survey B
Party 1	48,000	16,000
Party 2	36,000	22,000
Party 3	6,000	2,500
Party 4	2,000	6,000
Don't Know	8,000	3,500

a) In Survey A, what is the ratio of those intending to vote for Party 1 to those who responded 'Don't know'?

a) 12:1   b) 8:1   c) 6:1   d) 5:1   e) 4:1

b) In Survey B, what is the difference in the number of people intending to vote for Party 2 and Party 4?

a) 3,500   b) 14,000 c) 16,000 d) 19,500 e) 30,000

c) In Survey B, what percentage of people said they would vote for Party 3?

a) 5%   b) 10%   c) 15%   d) 20%   e) Can't tell

d) What is the difference between the two surveys in the percentage of people intending to vote for Party 4?

a) 2%   b) 4%   c) 8%   d) 10%   e) 12%

e) Which party is in the lead according to the survey results?

a) Party 1 b) Party 2 c) Party 3 d) Party 4 e) Can't tell

Answer sheet

	Mark the correct answer				
1a	a	b	c	d	e
1b	a	b	c	d	e
1c	a	b	c	d	e
1d	a	b	c	d	e
1e	a	b	c	d	e
2a	a	b	c	d	e
2b	a	b	c	d	e
2c	a	b	c	d	e
2d	a	b	c	d	e
2e	a	b	c	d	e
3a	a	b	c	d	e
3b	a	b	c	d	e
3c	a	b	c	d	e
3d	a	b	c	d	e
3e	a	b	c	d	e

University admissions tests

One of the growth areas for psychometric testing is in university admissions. This is a result of the enormous increase in popularity of some university courses, coupled with the increasing number of candidates who achieve top grades in their examinations. To put this in perspective, over the last five years the number of students applying to study medicine has increased by 88 per cent. And for medicine, and for that matter, dentistry, this means that the ratio of applications to acceptance is now approaching 10:1. Other courses such as veterinary science, law, and Oxbridge history, mathematics, physics and modern languages are also highly competitive.

The consequence is that admissions tests like the UK Clinical Aptitude Test (UKCAT), BioMedical Aptitude Test (BMAT) and Law National Admissions Test (LNAT), plus various Oxford and Cambridge tests, like the Thinking Skills Assessment (TSA), have been introduced. The results from these tests are used alongside other information, such as examination grades and personal statements, to make more balanced selection decisions.

The tests are designed to measure a variety of things. Some have an attainment component and rely on knowledge of a particular subject. For example, one of the questions in the BMAT practice paper is based on a diagram of the blood flow between the major organs of the human body. The task is to determine the path of the blood passing from the kidneys to the liver. Other tests, like the LNAT, have an essay section. In this you are asked to address a question such as: Sport is 'war minus the shooting'. Do you agree?

However what all these tests have in common is a critical thinking component. Indeed, the main part of the UKCAT is composed of four critical thinking sub-tests. What this means is that if you are to prepare for most university admissions tests it is wise to practise with the same sort of tests that are used to select graduates for jobs. Use the example tests in this book and visit some of the websites listed in Chapter 7.

Also, to give you an idea of what to expect, try the example test that follows. The questions are from the TSA which is used by many colleges at Cambridge University to help select students for computer science, natural sciences, engineering and economics courses.

Thinking Skills Assessment

What follows are six questions from the TSA demonstration test. For each question, five possible answers, A, B, C, D and E, are provided. Choose the **one** answer you consider is correct and record your choice on the answer sheet at the end of the section.

Time guideline: See how many questions you can do in **10 minutes**.

Start when you are ready.

1. Every motorist pays the same amount for road tax, regardless of how much they use the roads: someone who covers as little as 1,000 miles pays the same as someone who covers 20,000. This is unfair. Road tax should be scrapped and the money raised by an increase in the tax on car fuel. Making this change would ensure that those who use the roads more would pay more. This would not only be a fairer system, but could also bring in more revenue.

   Which of the following best illustrates the principle underlying the argument above?

   a) People should receive free medical treatment only if they cannot afford to pay for it.
   b) People who travel to work every day by train should pay a lower fare than those who travel only occasionally.
   c) People who earn more than double the average wage should be made to pay much higher charges for dental treatment.
   d) Television channels should be paid for by subscription so that only those people who watch them should be made to pay.
   e) Telephone charges should be higher for business customers than for domestic customers because they are using the system only to make money.

2. When a sky diver leaves the aircraft, they fall faster and faster until they reach a maximum steady speed known as terminal velocity. The sky diver falls at this speed until the parachute opens. The parachute slows them down until a much smaller steady speed is reached. This speed remains constant until the sky diver touches the ground.

Which of these graphs could show this information?

3. Jonathan is planning to use a 10 acre field to supply winter silage for his cattle and hay for his sheep. He reckons to get 100 bales of hay from each acre. Before cutting the hay he will first cut an acre round the edge of the field as silage – this allows him to manoeuvre his hay making machinery. After making his hay in June he will cut the whole field as second cut silage in August and again as third cut silage in September. His farm manual provides the following information.

	As silage	As hay
First cut	7 bales per acre	100 small bales per acre
Second cut	5 bales per acre	Not applicable
Third cut	4 bales per acre	Not applicable

How many bales of silage will Jonathan have at the end of his harvest?

a) 16
b) 90
c) 97
d) 157
e) 160

4. Tanya has 2 pigs. She estimates the weight of one as being 85 kg and the other as about 72 kg. She has ready access to a cheap source of potatoes but wishes to feed her pigs a 50/50 nutritional mix of potatoes and meal. Two tables from her feed book are reproduced below.

State of pig	Amount of meal to feed each day (for feeding meal alone)	Nutritional equivalents to 1 kg of meal	
80 kg – bacon weight	2.5 kg	Carrots	8 kg
60 kg–80 kg	2.0 kg	Comfrey	5 kg
50 kg – 60 kg	1.8 kg	Grass	5 kg
40 kg – 50 kg	1.6 kg	Kale	7 kg
30 kg – 40 kg	1.4 kg	Potatoes	5 kg
20 kg – 30 kg	1.0 kg	Skim milk	6 litres
Weaners: 8–10 weeks	Up to 1.0 kg	Swedes	8 kg
Weaners: 6 weeks to wearning	250–350 g	Whey	9–10 kg

How much meal should Tanya feed her pigs each day?

   a) 2.25 kg
   b) 2.50 kg
   c) 4.50 kg
   d) 11.25 kg
   e) 22.50 kg

5. Ever since Uranus was discovered in 1781, astronomers have thought there might be more planets to be discovered in the Solar System. Because of small deviations in the orbits of Uranus and Neptune – deviations which would occur if another planet existed – some astronomers think there must be an undiscovered planet – Planet X. But the search for Planet X is futile, because these deviations would occur if the orbits had been wrongly predicted. Since Uranus and Neptune take many decades to circle the sun, astronomers must rely on old data in order to calculate their orbits. If this data is inaccurate, the calculated orbits are wrong. If the calculated orbits are wrong, Uranus and Neptune will deviate from them even if there is no Planet X.

Which of the following is the best statement of the flaw in the argument above?

a) From the fact that the old data is inaccurate, it cannot be inferred that the calculated orbits are wrong.
b) From the fact that the data about the orbits is old it cannot be inferred that it is inaccurate.
c) From the fact that deviations occur which would occur if Planet X existed, it cannot be inferred that Planet X exists.
d) From the fact that the calculated orbits are wrong, it cannot be inferred that Uranus and Neptune will deviate from them.
e) From the fact that Planet X has not been discovered, it cannot be inferred that the search for it is futile.

6. The diagram shows a square piece of paper with identical semicircles cut out half way along three of its edges.

Which of the following is not a possible view of the paper after it has been folded along one of the dotted lines?

A

B

C

D

E

Answer sheet

	Mark the correct answer				
1	A	B	C	D	E
2	A	B	C	D	E
3	A	B	C	D	E
4	A	B	C	D	E
5	A	B	C	D	E
6	A	B	C	D	E

From the Thinking Skills Assessment
(*www.tsa.cambridgeassessment.org.uk*).
Reprinted by permission of the University of Cambridge Local
Examinations Syndicate.

Personality questionnaires

Personality, like ability, is a key influence on how a person performs at work. It's particularly important in all those situations that involve interaction and co-operation with other people; namely all managerial, supervisory, customer oriented, team or group based activities.

Personality is usually measured by using a self-report questionnaire. This is a 'test' that directly asks *you* about aspects of your own personality, allowing for a consistent and objective measure of things like how you cope with pressure, your preferred way of dealing with other people and your general behavioural style. In this way personality is really the characteristic way in which you respond to situations, or your preferred way of behaving in particular circumstances, or towards other people.

It has recently been estimated that there are 1,200 self-report questionnaires on the UK market alone, and that they are used by over 50 per cent of medium- to large-sized organizations. Their popularity is no doubt due to the speedy and objective way in which they can give a detailed picture of what a person is like, and the ease with which this 'profile' can be matched against the *behavioural* requirements of a job. However, whatever the use, it's important that the aspect of personality that is measured is genuinely part of you, rather than merely the consequence of a particular situation; and also something that allows predictions to be made across a range of different activities. For example, knowing that you are an extrovert, but that you behave in completely different ways in different social situations, wouldn't be of much use.

Another critical thing about personality is that it does not change dramatically over time. This does not mean that it never changes, rather that it's stable enough to be measured in a meaningful way. Again, it wouldn't be very useful to ask you to complete a questionnaire one day, only to get a completely different result if you did the same questionnaire a week later. This is obviously rather important from an employer's point of view as employment is a long-term business. As such it's valuable to know how you are likely to behave over the months and years you will be with a particular organization, not just on the day you happen to have been tested.

To summarize, personality questionnaires are a standard and objective way of discovering your preferred ways of behaving and relating to other people. They allow an employer to see if you fit the behavioural requirements of a particular job; or, conversely, if you're already in a job, to identify your training and development needs. From a purely selfish point of view they also allow you to 'choose' work that better suits you temperamentally, and which you will find more interesting and satisfying.

Different personality questionnaires

There are many different designs of personality questionnaire, but the vast majority fall into only one of two psychological camps. These are those that assign you to a specific personality *type,* and those that are based on a *trait* approach – a trait being an aspect of personality that you possess to a lesser or greater extent.

Type questionnaires

There are a number of commonly used personality question-naires that are based on a type approach, yet they all owe their basic structure to the work of the Swiss psychologist Carl Jung. He developed a theory to describe the *predictable* differences between the ways in which people behave in different situations. The crux of his argument was that the variations in our behaviour are caused by the way we prefer to use our minds. The use of the word 'prefer' is important here because the Jungian approach is rooted in an either/or way of looking at personality, ie you take this approach *or* that approach, not a bit of both.

In terms of preference, the two options we have when our minds are active are to receive information (perceiving), or to process it and come to a decision (judging). Moreover, if the focus is on perceiving, then there are only two ways of taking on board information, sensing and intuition; likewise, judging splits into thinking and feeling. Thus, there are four key processes that we use to understand the world around us, the only further modification being our orientation towards the world, either extroverted or introverted. The former shows a concern for social interaction with other people, and a desire to understand and experience the world at large. The latter shows a fascination for the 'inner world' of thinking, feeling and reflecting.

To summarize, the type approach allows your personality preferences to be expressed on 4 double-ended scales, giving a total of 16 main types. However, that's not to say that you're 'stuck' with one of 16 particular ways of behaving, rather that you have a natural and comfortable way of behaving. An analogy that is often used is that of having to write with your 'wrong' hand. If you do this it feels unnatural and clumsy, and requires concentration, whereas if you use your preferred hand your writing is automatic and you don't have to think about it. In the same way we all have a definite preference, say, for perceiving or judging; and if we are able to use our preferred approach we are generally more confident *and* competent.

This method of personality classification does not imply that there are 'good' or 'bad' personalities. Thus, 'extrovert' does not equal 'good with other people', or 'introvert' 'shy' and 'retiring'. People simply differ in their approaches and, if you happen to have a similar approach to another person, you will tend to share similar sorts of behaviours and attitudes. These may be more or less useful, strengths or limitations, depending on what you are trying to do. The other thing to realize is that type can be independent of ability, in that the sort of 'intelligence' you have does not dictate the sort of person you are.

The type approach is mostly used in an intrapersonal sense, that is for development and exploration of the self. It can also be used to select people for jobs, but usually only if the questionnaire is designed so that direct comparisons can be made between people in terms of the *amounts* of particular characteristics they possess (a normative approach – see Chapter 1). This being said, questionnaires based on the type system are completed by millions of people every year. In consequence it makes sense to spend a little more time exploring the 'preferences' in more detail.

Extroversion–introversion

Extroverted people are concerned with the world that surrounds them. They like to interact with other people, and are fond of talking and debating. In social situations they tend to take the initiative, and to search out other people. However, sometimes their enthusiasm leads them to say things without thinking, and they may inadvertently hurt others. In a work context, extroverts are active and people oriented; and they do not like slow, repetitive jobs.

Those who are introverted tend to be more involved in their own private world. They like to analyse what they are going to say before they say it, and may prefer to communicate in writing. There is a 'self-contained' air to their dealings with other people, and they may sometimes be regarded as being a little too cool and detached. At work introverts need quiet so that they can concentrate (they don't like open-plan offices), and are quite happy to work alone.

Judging–perceiving

Those who prefer a judging style live in a structured and orderly way. They like to have plans and schedules, and work to a timetable. Their whole life is organized, controlled, and executed in a precise manner. In the workplace they need order and a plan of action, and work best when they can organize their time thoroughly. They also like to follow a task through to an obvious and tangible conclusion.

In contrast the perceiving person reacts in a flexible and spontaneous manner, and adapts to what is going on rather than attempting to control it. This casual approach often manifests itself in last-minute planning and an 'open-ended' approach to life. Unlike the judging person, the perceiver feels positively claustrophobic if things are planned to the last detail. At work this can cause problems, especially with jobs that need to be completed within tight deadlines. However, many perceiving people would claim that they produce their best work at the eleventh hour!

Sensing–intuition

This aspect of personality is concerned with how you prefer to receive information, with sensing people concentrating on the information that flows from their senses of sight, hearing, taste, touch and smell. Such people are usually practically oriented and assess things in a step-by-step way. They tend to trust what they sense, and are rooted in the 'here and now'. In the work context, this manifests itself in a preference for dealing with facts, and sensing people can usually be relied upon to be right about matters of detail.

The intuitive person has a more abstract approach and is

interested in the interconnections between things, not necessarily the things themselves. The concern is more with the 'big picture' and how information fits together in different patterns. Indeed, the truly intuitive person may be particularly good at developing new insights and working out different ways of doing things. From a work point of view this means that intuitive types tend to follow their noses, and may actually overlook certain facts. There is also a tendency to work in short, inspirational bursts, rather than make steady, continuous progress.

Thinking–feeling

A preference for thinking indicates a detached and logical approach to problem solving. The style is characterized by the search for cause and effect, and a reduction of situations to their component parts. There is little room for fancy, and such an analytic and impersonal style is perhaps best described as 'scientific' (and for fans of the TV programme *Star Trek* is perhaps most akin to the Vulcan objectivity of Mr Spock). At work the thinker is firm minded and principled, but may tend to overlook the human side of things.

In stark contrast the feeling person bases decisions on their likely impact on other people. The mentality is one of identifying with the thoughts and feelings of others, and of adopting the most sympathetic approach. This is sometimes described as 'tender-mindedness', as the aim of any action is to take the most compassionate line. Thus, feeling individuals are distinguished by their understanding and supportive style, and are usually driven by a strong sense of the value of the individual. In a work scenario this translates into a desire to please other people, and to ensure a harmonious working environment.

Questionnaire formats

The questions in a personality questionnaire can be presented in a number of different ways. A format that is often used in type questionnaires is one that forces you to choose between two options, or to rank a number of statements in terms of how true they are of you.

Example 1: Forced Choice
Do you prefer to:
(a) plan what you do in advance; or
(b) react to things as they happen?

If you answered (b) to the above question you would be saying that you like to wait and see what happens rather than organize yourself before events. That's because the two parts of the question score on different personality scales. However, the big problem with this approach is that you have not been able to indicate how true you believe *either* of the statements to be. In reality you may be neither very organized nor very reactive; indeed you may be a combination of both depending on the circumstances. What this means is that tests constructed in this way can only broadly comment on you as an individual; and they cannot (unless used very judiciously) be applied to selection situations. The following example should make this point even clearer.

Example 2: Ranking
Rank in order of interest, 1 to 3, the following sports:
Golf   [ ]
Football   [ ]
Tennis   [ ]

Supposing we both answered *Example 2*, we might both order the sports (1) Tennis, (2) Golf, (3) Football. However, in practice, you might be a professional tennis player and a keen golfer, and I might just enjoy watching them all on the television. So what this sort of approach cannot do is show the strength and application of a particular interest or, in the personality sense, the different amounts of a particular characteristic. This is a very important consideration for employers who are interested in the relative balance of characteristics between potential employees.

How are type questionnaires used?

Type questionnaires are widely used in organizations for development and training purposes. They can help to show the sort of environments in which people prefer to work, the way in which they are likely to go about their work, and the ideal personality of any colleagues with whom they would work best. This last concern has become more important in recent years with the increase in work teams, groups or cells. Indeed, the team approach is now common in most areas of employment from manufacturing plants, such as those producing cars and aircraft, to retail businesses like banks, supermarkets and shops.

By far the most widely used type questionnaire is the *Myers–Briggs Type Indicator®* (*MBTI®*), with over 3.5 million people taking it throughout the world each year. It is published by Consulting Psychologist Press Inc in the USA, and is also available from Oxford Psychologists Press in the UK. Other type questionnaires include the *Type Dynamics Indicator* from Team Focus Ltd, the *Jung Type Indicator*, published by Psytech International Ltd, and the *Occupational Type Profile* produced by Selby Millsmith Ltd.

Trait questionnaires

Trait questionnaires are concerned with the differing amounts of personality characteristics that all people possess. So these questionnaires are designed to measure how much of a certain trait you possess, eg how extroverted you are compared to another candidate for a job, or how stable you are compared to people in general. The traits that are measured are assumed to influence the ways in which we behave, and so are predictive of behaviour. Indeed, those who design questionnaires that measure traits, such as the famous American psychologist Raymond Cattell, have defined personality as 'that which permits a prediction of what a person will do in a given situation'. However, before we move on to look at the different sorts of traits that can be measured, it is useful to think about the difference between a trait and a state. This isn't just of academic interest as it's important that a questionnaire is measuring a stable and enduring aspect of a person's personality, rather than just the current state of that person. After all, we pass through different mental states during the day, with our mood changes depending on the situations in which we find ourselves. Naturally, most questionnaires attempt to concentrate on the measurement of traits, but there are some that assess both trait and state. Thus, whether or not you are an anxious person can be measured, alongside an indication of whether or not you were anxious at the time you completed the questionnaire.

There are about 20,000 words in the English language that label traits. Obviously many of these relate to the same underlying traits, but even so that still leaves a considerable range of different characteristics. As such it should come as no surprise that questionnaires have been designed that measure anything from 3 to 30 or more aspects of personality. This may sound confusing but not all questionnaires are attempting to measure every part of someone's personality, and many are actually concentrating on what are recognized as the five key dimensions of personality. These are known as the 'Big Five', or the 'Five Factor Model', and are reckoned to be the primary personality dimensions that underpin all observable behaviour! I should say, however, that there isn't universal agreement on this question and many psychologists would argue that there are as few as three main dimensions. This being said, the 'Big Five' are worth exploring in some detail. Incidentally, along the way you will notice that there are some similarities with the type descriptions given in the last section, demonstrating that both type and trait approaches are covering more or less the same ground.

The 'Big Five'

A great deal of research points to the fact that personality can be broken down into five main dimensions or domains. These concern how people approach situations and tasks (action); the style of their reasoning (thinking); how they behave towards other people (relating); the underlying nature of their emotions (feeling); and how they regulate their actions (conformity).

Action

This concerns an individual's attitude towards other people in a work or personal context. In many questionnaires it is either referred to as 'tough-mindedness' or as 'agreeableness'. The tough-minded person is someone who is primarily results orientated, and who may disregard other people's feelings in pursuit of a particular goal. Those who are very tough-minded have little time or patience for those who need support, and tend to work best with other like-minded colleagues.

It is, of course, possible to possess the complementary personality characteristics and be a tender-minded person. This suggests a warmer, more people-focused individual who has a genuine concern for the feelings of other people. This sort of person is also more likely to achieve results by listening to different viewpoints, and to adopt a co-operative, trusting and consensual style. In this way those wishing to discuss sensitive and personal issues are far more likely to approach this sort of person than their tough-minded, results-driven counterpart.

Thinking

This is about the structure and organization a person brings to a situation. It also relates to self-discipline and, characteristically, to attention to detail. The 'structured' person places great value on order and control. This manifests itself in a very tidy and systematic way of approaching tasks. For example, projects are often planned to the last detail, and organized in a precise and meticulous manner. Thus, a highly structured person leaves nothing to chance, and is always conscious of what to do and how long it will take. In extreme cases this can appear somewhat obsessional (especially to a 'low structure' individual), or overly perfectionist.

A 'low structure' person tends to have a more relaxed and casual approach to life. As long as jobs are completed, such people do not worry about formal structures or schedules. They are not particularly concerned with personal organization and can sometimes appear somewhat disorganized. In many cases they may miss important details or, because they are less ordered, be late for appointments or meetings. In a managerial sense they have a greater preference for the overview or the strategic approach, rather than the detail or tactical level of a project.

Relating

Classically, this refers to how a person relates to other people in the environment. It is the personality dimension that is most used by the layperson when describing other people as it concerns extroversion and introversion.

The extroverted individual is sociable, outgoing and attracted to other people. Such a person is energetic and enthusiastic, and is prepared to voice an opinion and to become involved in most things. At work, people-centred and high-profile roles have the most appeal, especially those relying on the skills of negotiation and persuasion. However, extroverts can be rather impulsive and sometimes take risks without properly weighing up the odds. They can at times also appear rather domineering, and find it difficult to believe that others do not share the same enthusiasms they do.

The introverted character is less concerned with other people and tends to be more introspective. In general there is a less excitable and more moderate outlook, and a tendency to take a more cautious and restrained approach to work. Introverts are also far less likely to want to be 'in charge' or to seek the limelight. In many ways the attitude is one of personal challenge (the inner game), rather than an open competition with other people. In terms of analogy it's like wishing to break a personal best time in athletics, rather than race against other people.

Feeling

This relates to the level of confidence you have as an individual. It is sometimes also referred to as neuroticism, anxiety or emotionality. However, basically it concerns how self-assured you are as a person.

Those with high self-confidence tend to be relaxed and optimistic. They enjoy responsibility and like to be put to the test. When they are put under pressure they react in a calm and organized way, and have faith in their own ability to cope. At work they are able to deal with unexpected events with ease, and put their views forward with confidence and conviction. Other people are likely to see them as being highly personally competent and assertive.

Those with low confidence, or high emotionality, have difficulty coping with stress and pressure. While they *can* take on responsibility, they may find it places a considerable emotional strain on them. They also tend to question their abilities, and are generally more pessimistic and cautious than those who are confident. In the work sense they prefer predictability and tend to shy away from complex, open-ended situations. This suggests that routine jobs in large, supportive organizations are likely to suit them the best.

Conformity

This refers to a person's need for variety, or the way in which an individual responds to change. It is also sometimes called creativity, independence or openness to experience.

The conforming person works within existing rules and regulations, and usually deals with problems using well-established methods. The approach is measured and conservative, and can be described as being 'by the book'. Such individuals are also practically minded and more comfortable with implementing plans rather than creating them. The conforming person is happy operating within the status quo and does not have a burning ambition to be seen as creative.

In contrast the non-conforming person is concerned with individual expression. This frequently indicates an unconventional and creative thinker, who actually resents structure and order. Thus, non-conforming people actively seek out and enjoy discovering new ways of doing things, and like to have variety in their work. At work the non-conformer is seen as being innovative and change oriented. There is a resistance to the traditional way of doing things, and a preference for risk taking. The latter can sometimes prove dangerous for an organization as uncontrolled risk taking can lead to business failure. However, modern management thinkers do suggest that some non-conforming people are desirable in an organization as they provide the catalyst for change or, as it is sometimes described, the grit in the oyster. This is a useful expression as it's the grit that ultimately leads to the pearl.

Trait questions

There are two main ways in which the questions in trait questionnaires are arranged. These involve either rating a list of statements, or indicating choices between a number of statements.

Example 3: Rating
Mark the [1] if you strongly agree with the statement; the [2] if you agree; the [3] if you are unsure; the [4] if you disagree; and the [5] if you strongly disagree.

1. I enjoy social gatherings   [1] [2] [3] [4] [5]
2. I am always late for appointments [1] [2] [3] [4] [5]
3. I avoid taking risks   [1] [2] [3] [4] [5]
4. I like playing team games   [1] [2] [3] [4] [5]

Note: Sometimes the questions appear in the form of lists of adjectives (creative, dominant, tense, active, social, sensitive etc), rather than statements. In this case all you do is indicate your level of agreement, 1–5, with a series of words.

Example 4: Two from four choice
For each block of four statements indicate which one is most like you [M], and which one is least like you [L]. Leave the other two statements blank.

I am ...
1. A highly organized person   [M]   [L]
   Anxious when meeting new people   [M]   [L]
   The 'life and soul' of the party   [M]   [L]
   An energetic person   [M]   [L]
2. Even tempered   [M]   [L]
   Skilled at practical problems   [M]   [L] etc

Example 5: One from two choice
For each statement indicate whether you think it is true [T] or false [F]:

1. I like to try new ways of doing things   [T]   [F]
2. I find it difficult to relax after a hard day's work [T]   [F]
3. I am an optimistic person   [T]   [F]
4. I enjoy organizing meetings and gatherings   [T]   [F]

Example 6: One from three choice
For each statement indicate whether you think the statement is true [T]; false [F]; or if you are unsure [?]:

1. People should sort out their own problems [T] [?] [F]
2. I can get more done when I can work alone [T] [?] [F]
3. I like telling people funny stories   [T] [?] [F]
4. I show my emotions easily   [T] [?] [F]

All the above are common ways of presenting questions and, as you can see, some allow more choice than others. In particular one of the biggest differences is between those questionnaires that allow you to respond 'unsure' [?], and those that force your choice between a number of options. You may feel that you don't want to be forced to answer one way or the other; however, questionnaires are designed like this to stop you being indifferent to everything. That's because if you were unsure, or couldn't make your mind up about most of the statements in a questionnaire, it would be impossible to produce an accurate picture of your personality.

How are trait questionnaires used?

Trait questionnaires are used for selection and development purposes. Unlike type questionnaires they can be used to select people for jobs because they allow an employer directly to compare one person with another. Therefore it is possible to say that person A is more extroverted than person B, and also how much more extroverted A is than B.

Questionnaires of this design are used in most of the large companies in the UK and the USA. Variations are also available in most European and Asian countries, translated into the appropriate languages. Virtually all measure the 'Big Five' personality dimensions, although in practice they usually do this by breaking the five main components down into a number of sub-scales. So, for example, in the UK, the most popular questionnaires contain 16 and 32 scales respectively.

The names to look out for are the *Sixteen Personality Factor Questionnaire*™ (*16PF*), published in the UK by Oxford Psychologist Press; *People Mapper* from ASE; the *Occupational Personality Questionnaire*® (*OPQ*®), published by Saville & Holdsworth Ltd; and the *California Psychological Inventory*™ (*CPI*™), published by the Consulting Psychologists Press Inc, and distributed by Oxford Psychologists Press. Other questionnaires you might come across are the *Rapid Personality Questionnaire* (*RPQ*), *Manchester Personality Questionnaire* (*MPQ*), *Personal Profile Analysis* (*PPA*), and the *NEO Five Factor Inventory*™ (*NEO-FF*™). The first two were designed in the UK, while the others have their antecedents in the USA but are also widely used in the UK.

Emotional Intelligence

An additional development in personality assessment is the Emotional Intelligence (EI) questionnaire. This looks at the traits that are thought to differentiate between average and high performers in a work setting. What this really means is a person's emotional and interpersonal competence, or how we 'manage' our own personality. One way of looking at it, is that EI is the practice of 'thinking about feeling' *and* 'feeling about thinking'. EI questionnaires measure things like:

- **Self-awareness:** our understanding of our own feelings and how we control them.
- **Emotional resilience:** our ability to perform under pressure and to adapt to new situations.
- **Motivation:** the drive and energy we have to achieve results and to work towards goals.
- **Interpersonal sensitivity:** the degree of respect we have for others' needs.
- **Influence and persuasion:** our ability to bring other people around to our point of view.
- **Intuitiveness:** the process of being able to come to a clear decision when we only have incomplete or ambiguous information.
- **Conscientiousness and integrity:** our ability to display commitment and match words with action.

The traits measured by EI questionnaires have been chosen because they are predictive of likely success in given roles, particularly in the management arena. However, many are measured by standard personality questionnaires (albeit in the 'being' rather than the 'doing' sense), and they also have much in common with some of the 'competencies' described at the end of this book – see the Appendix.

As an example of the output from an EI questionnaire, read the following extract from a real report:

> While generally aware of your feelings and emotions in work situations, there are some situations in which this is not so. You might find that occasionally, even though you are aware of your feelings and emotions, you are unable to control their impact on the way in which you behave as much as you would like. In order to develop this element further, you might find it helpful to reflect on specific situations in which you have felt in control of your feelings and emotions. In thinking about these situations you may be able to identify specific actions that were helpful. You could then apply these in a broader situation that arouses strong feelings and emotions. (Emotional Intelligence Questionnaire report, ASE)

Having read the extract above, you will see that the report describes a person's typical behaviour and also provides some pointers on how to develop self-awareness.

There are many EI questionnaires on the market, including an option with the *Occupational Personality Questionnaire®* from Saville & Holdsworth Ltd; the *Emotional Intelligence Questionnaire* from ASE; and the *Emotional Competence Inventory* from HayGroup.

Personality and the 'dark side'

Finally, one of the latest ideas in personality is to look at personality disorders and to see how these relate to 'normal' functioning. For example, problems often arise if a person is too arrogant, melodramatic, aloof, or even perfectionist. But that's not to say that a small measure of some of these attributes cannot be good – it's when there is too much of one of them that things can go wrong. This, in the current jargon, can be potentially *derailing*.

Questionnaires like the *Hogan Development Survey* (HDS), distributed by the Psychological Consultancy Ltd, aim to measure these derailing factors, or what is also termed, the 'dark side' of personality. The HDS has 11 scales and looks at things like Enthusiastic – Volatile, Shrewd – Mistrustful,

Careful – Cautious, Vivacious – Dramatic, and so forth. Note that the words on the left-hand side of each scale are generally thought to indicate positive attributes; those on the right, what this attribute turns into when it's in excess.

To help to make the point, let's look at two 'flawed' personality types which link to an HDS scale. Histrionic people need to be the centre of attention and enjoy making a drama out of any sort of crisis. What's more, they often demonstrate seductive, and often provocative behaviour in their dealings with other people. They also tend to look and dress the part, and use exaggerated expressions of emotion. You may recognize this description as being like that of the melodramatic theatrical 'luvvie'. Unfortunately it is also sometimes attached to those in managerial and leadership roles.

The obsessive–compulsive type is totally obsessed with details, plans, rules and schedules. They are sticklers for doing things 'right' and their perfectionism often gets in the way of things that need to be done. Such people are often workaholics and highly driven, and so can be of genuine benefit to an organization. However too much attention to detail can mean that they find it difficult to delegate, and come across as highly controlling. There are many bosses like this and they can be difficult to work for, not least because someone who spends an excessive amount of time at work often thinks that other people should do likewise.

So in short, 'dark side' personality questionnaires are attempting to measure the type of dysfunctional behaviour that erodes the trust, loyalty and enthusiasm that is critical to successful management and leadership.

How to complete a personality questionnaire

At present, most personality questionnaires come in the form of a question book and a separate answer sheet. Thus, your task is simply to read the questions and complete the answer sheet using a pencil. However, many questionnaires are becoming available on computer and so you may find yourself using a keyboard to respond to questions presented on a computer screen. There are also a number of other less common variations (see Chapter 2), but irrespective of how the questions are physically presented they will always be in one of the formats described previously. In addition, it's worth remembering that if you are tested by computer you will not be expected to be a keyboard expert (it's your personality that is being assessed, not your typing skills); and you will always have the opportunity to practise and to ask questions before the assessment begins.

There follows some general guidelines on how to approach any personality questionnaire:

- **Be as honest as you can.** The best advice is to give the most straightforward answer to any question. Do not look for trick questions or be tempted to give the answers you feel will do you the most good, but which are untrue. The reasons are that it is difficult to 'bend the truth' consistently when you may be answering up to 200 questions; and you may also inadvertently emphasize one aspect of your personality at the expense of another. Likewise, you do not know the ideal profile for a particular job, and you may actually distort your personality results in the wrong direction.

  In addition, many questionnaires contain special scales that are designed to detect those who are presenting themselves in an overly positive light. These are called 'impression management' or 'motivational distortion' scales, and contain questions to check how honest and consistent you are being. For example:

  I have never been late for an appointment   True   False
  I have never told a 'white lie'   True   False

Some questionnaires also contain scales that can help to identify potential criminal behaviour, or addictive personalities. Clearly such information can be of value to employers in the retail and financial sectors, although it should be stressed that no questionnaire can produce a foolproof indication of such behaviour. This being the case they are always backed up by other sources of information, eg personal references.

● **Think about a typical day.** The questions you will be asked relate to how you usually behave at work. If you don't have a job just think about how you deal with other people in social situations, or how you deal with situations at school, college, or wherever you spend your time.

● **Trust your first impressions.** Although most questionnaires have no time limit, it is better to answer the questions quickly rather than agonize over each one. The reason is that in this case, unlike ability tests, your first thoughts are usually the most accurate. It's also a good idea to work quickly because it will often take you between 30 and 40 minutes to finish a questionnaire even when you are trusting your first impressions. That's not to say that every questionnaire will take this long, as some are quite short, and will only take about 10 minutes to finish. The latter are often used to recruit people for customer service or sales positions.

● **Read the questions carefully.** If you study the questions it is often possible to determine which broad aspects of personality are being measured. For example, extroversion or *relating* questions frequently refer to sociability, risk-taking, impulsiveness, lack of responsibility and high levels of emotional energy. In contrast, introversion questions often cover the opposite characteristics such as a dislike for social occasions and more thoughtful decision making.

In a similar vein, tough-mindedness or *action* questions often concern achievement orientation, competitiveness, assertiveness, manipulation and a lack of sympathy for other people, whereas tender-mindedness questions focus on a feeling, trusting and co-operative style, or on an empathic way of behaving.

Likewise, questions concerning anxiety or *feeling* will be based on issues such as low self-esteem, obsessive behaviour (such as repeatedly checking things or always having to be early for appointments) and a lack of personal autonomy. The contrasting confidence questions will concern things like being able to respond in crises, being able to take criticism, not worrying over mistakes, and generally taking a relaxed view of life.

The thinking or *structure* questions will relate to how organized a person is in everyday life. So high-structure questions will tap behaviours such as ordering and controlling people and things, and anything relating to detailed planning and organising tasks in advance. The low-structure items will then cover a dislike for organization and planning, and especially things like a poor sense of time or lack of personal discipline.

Finally, *conformity* questions will concern practicality, conservatism, tried-and-tested methods and conscientiousness. Their low-conformity counterparts will cover creative and divergent thinking, a frustration with rules and regulations, a need to be able to express individuality, and a search for variety and mental stimulation.

In describing the content of questions like this, the argument is that if you understand what the questions are asking, you will be able to give better and more genuine responses.

- **Answer all the questions.** It's important that you answer all the questions or it will not be possible to get a valid picture of your personality. Also, don't get stuck on questions you don't feel are relevant, but just give the best and most immediate answer you can. A related problem is 'arguing' with the questions, ie over-analysing the questions to such an extent that you don't know what is being asked. Unfortunately, some questions will appear rather ambiguous but, as before, the most profitable thing to do is just give your first reaction.

- **Know yourself.** The more self-knowledge you have the easier it will be to present an accurate picture. Remember that personality questionnaires are really only asking you to report on yourself, and so it makes sense to be as aware as you can of your own personality. You can do this by consulting self-test books (look in a good bookshop), or by asking other people to describe how they see you. In fact, one of the most interesting things you can do is to write down, say, 10 adjectives that you feel sum up your personality, and then get someone who knows you well to do the same thing. If you then compare the two lists you may get a few surprises!

- **Know the job.** Just as it's useful to know something about your personality before you complete a questionnaire, it's also beneficial to know about the job for which you are applying. What sort of a person are they looking for? You will get some clues from the job advertizement and also any other literature you can study before the assessment session. For example, you may find that an advert refers to particular 'competencies' (see the Appendix for more details), or that a company publishes a house magazine or newsletter. Do these give a feel for the ideal employee? What impression do you get of the organization? Perhaps it's large and traditional, and favours 'middle-of-the-road', detail-conscious and stable workers. Or is it small, fast moving and creative? Does this suggest more dynamic, risk-taking and extroverted individuals?

Finally, always follow the directions printed in the front of the questionnaire booklet, and pay particular attention to any instructions given by the test administrator. It should also be a comfort to remember that personality questionnaires are designed to assess you in a fair and objective way, and to help you choose the work to which you are most suited. Clearly there's little point in fulfilling all the requirements of a job in terms of ability and experience, only to find that you cannot cope with the people aspects of a particular position.

Leadership Style questionnaire

To provide some experience of completing a self-report questionnaire what follows is a fully working Leadership Style questionnaire. This is based on the work of Daniel Goleman and the Hay Group into what characterizes highly effective leaders, in particular the six distinct managerial styles. Effective managers use a combination of these styles, at the appropriate time, to build a positive working environment for their teams.

Practice questionnaire

Introduction
The Leadership Style Questionnaire (LSQ) contains 30 pairs of statements. The statements ask about how you think, feel and deal with the people with whom you work. When you have completed the questionnaire you will be able to identify the sort of style, or styles, that you use when managing or leading other people.

Instructions
For each question decide which of the two statements is most like you. Then put a cross in the appropriate box.

Example

		A	B	C	D	E	F
1.	I feel that people should always be involved in decisions, or						
	I expect people to do what I have told them do				**X**		

When you answer the questions, bear the following points in mind:

- Try and be as honest as you can when answering the questions.
- Don't spend too long thinking about each question; just give the first answer that comes into your mind.
- Make sure that you answer all of the questions, even if some of the statements are difficult to choose between.
- There is no time limit, but try to complete the questionnaire as quickly as you can.
- Don't look at the scoring system until you have completed the questionnaire!

Start when you are ready.

		A	B	C	D	E	F
1.	I think the key to success is through meeting peoples needs, or I like to give people a clear direction to follow						
2.	I help people to identify their strengths and weaknesses, or I insist on excellence						
3.	I think that you need to tell people what to do, or I include everyone in decision making						
4.	I am good at selling a 'vision' of where we need to go, or I encourage people to work on their own development needs						
5.	I concentrate on promoting harmony amongst people, or I prefer to lead by example						
6.	I give people feedback on their work performance, or I expect people to do what I say						
7.	I organize meetings to decide what needs to be done, or I think that my main job is to complete things to a high standard						
8.	I pay attention to the whole person and their happiness, or I tailor my support to the needs of the individual						
9.	I persuade people by explaining what needs to be done, or I trust people to work out how to do their job						
10.	I closely monitor the work that people are doing, or I often find that to get something done I have to do it myself						

		A	B	C	D	E	F
11.	I am good at listening to other people, or						
	I reward the whole team if it has done well						
12.	I give people constructive feedback, or						
	I get people to comply instantly because it raises standards						
13.	I always look for opportunities to give positive feedback, or						
	I prefer to reach decisions by consensus						
14.	I provide a clear idea of long term direction, or						
	I only delegate to people I know will do a good job						
15.	I reward the person as much as their job performance, or						
	I think people need to know exactly what is expected of them						
16.	I believe in creating a warm and caring atmosphere, or						
	I let people know when they are doing well						
17.	I think that you sometimes need to learn from failure, or						
	I take responsibility away from people who do not perform						
18.	I insist on procedures so that people know what to do, or						
	I believe in building commitment from all involved						
19.	I delegate tasks to people with clear instructions, or						
	I help people to see that learning is a continuous process						
20.	I see my role as looking after other people, or						
	I think that you often have to demonstrate how to do things well						

		A	B	C	D	E	F
21.	I take time to discover people's aspirations for the future, or						
	I think that you must always keep on top of what is going on						
22.	I believe in involving everyone in issues affecting them, or						
	I give people precise details on what to do						
23.	I want people to feel valued as individuals, or						
	I look for opportunities to enhance people's development						
24.	I set standards which everyone can understand, or						
	I am good at organizing and running meetings						
25.	I think people respect you if you can also do their job well, or						
	I set high standards and expect others to reach them						
26.	I think the main thing is people's long term development, or						
	I am concerned with getting everyone's contribution						
27.	I ask people for their ideas on how to achieve goals, or						
	I think people need to be told when they are not doing well						
28.	I believe that to work together we must all like each other, or						
	I wait until everyone has had their say before making decisions						
29.	I am good at explaining the 'big picture' to people, or						
	I always act to put things right as quickly as possible						
30.	I think that welfare comes before organizational goals, or						
	I swiftly point out when people have deviated from the rules						

Scoring the questionnaire

Simply add up all the crosses in each of the six columns, A–F, and record the totals in the table below.

Column	Total	Style
A		Affiliative
B		Authoritative
C		Coaching
D		Coercive
E		Democratic
F		Pace-setting

What the styles mean

The styles show you what you think you do as a manager or leader, and what you consider to be important. Look at the one or two styles with the highest total scores. What do the results tell you? Should you use these styles less? Contrast with the style with the lowest score: is this an area for development? Should you use this style more?

Affiliative

This is all about creating a peaceful and harmonious working environment and building strong emotional bonds with other people. It rests on empathy, paying attention to relationships and good communication skills. It's useful when there are fault lines in teams, or to motivate people during difficult periods.

Overall it has a positive effect on organizational 'climate' in that it frees people to be more creative, increases sense of ownership and responsibility, clarity of purpose and commitment. However one possible problem is that it can often look like avoiding the difficult problems, especially those concerned with poor performance.

Authoritative

An authoritative approach is concerned with selling a 'vision'. It relies on self-confidence, a persuasive style, and the ability to act as a catalyst of change. It comes into its own when change requires a new vision of the future, or when a clear and unambiguous direction is needed.

In terms of climate this has the most strongly positive effect and is the style to adopt for maximum impact on the working atmosphere. If there is a downside it's that it can sometimes backfire when team members are highly competent and capable, and they actually know best!

Coaching

This focuses on developing people for the future. The underlying emotional competencies are empathy, self-awareness and a concern for empowering others to grow and develop. It is of particular value when the concern is over improving performance and on developing long-term strengths and capability.

As with the Affiliative and Authoritative styles it has a positive effect on organizational climate. Yet it should be recognized that the coach sometimes needs to trade a short term drop in performance for a long term increase in capability.

Coercive

This is about compliance and getting others to immediately do what they are told. It is driven by the need to achieve, self-control and initiative and is the style that works best when there is a crisis, or when a problem needs a kick-start.

It should be used sparingly because in terms of climate it has a negative effect. It can stifle creativity and decrease sense of ownership and responsibility. It's also not particularly useful when the need is to communicate the 'big picture' or a guiding strategy.

Democratic

The democratic style is about deciding things together and creating a sense of common purpose. It draws on the competencies of collaboration, communication and team building. This style is useful when there is a need to get people to buy in to a course of action, or to get the right sort of input from the most capable members of a team.

In terms of climate it's another style that has a positive effect, alongside the Authoritative and Affiliative approaches. However it's not a good style to use in a crisis when there is no time for meetings or discussions.

Pace-setting

This centres on standards and is mostly concerned with setting targets for performance. The underpinning competencies are conscientiousness, drive to achieve and initiative. It works best where there is a need to get quick results from a team that is already highly motivated and competent.

Along with the coercive style this is one that should be used on a limited basis. It should be recognized that it is a quick fix and not a style that will help teams to deliver to a high standard over the long term.

Other self-report questionnaires

There are a number of other aspects of human temperament that can be measured apart from personality. These include qualities such as values, motivation, integrity and interests. All of these additional factors are assessed at one time or another, and the next section deals with each in more detail.

Values

These are the 'personal concepts' that we hold, which determine how we deal with everyday life. They are the standards or principles that guide our behaviour towards other people. In practice, of course, it's difficult to differentiate between values and aspects of personality; but, unlike personality, values are influenced more by the culture in which we live.

Values questionnaires are often used to complement personality assessments, and are usually focused on how you cope with everyday problems and/or your relationships with other people.

The questionnaires are generally designed in a forced-choice format (see Example 1: Forced Choice) and measure values such as:

- honesty;
- self-respect;
- equality;
- goal orientation;
- self-control;
- independence;
- altruism;
- social support.

Values questionnaires are often used in assessment programmes for middle and senior managers. The best-known example is probably the *Global Gordon's Personal Profile Inventory (Global GPP-I)* distributed by ASE.

Motivation

Motivation is closely related to the issue of values and is one of the most important things to assess during the selection process. However, it's also one of the hardest to measure as we all claim to be highly motivated when we apply for jobs; in particular we are likely to put on a great show of interest during the interview.

In practice, motivation can be defined as the energy that we are likely to bring to bear on work tasks. This is useful for an employer to know as it is essential to select people who are genuinely motivated, and committed to making a success of a job. It's also important to know what a person wishes to strive towards, and those activities or circumstances that both increase *and* decrease motivation.

Motivation questionnaires are often used with managerial, professional and supervisory staff, and aim to identify the range of factors that energize and support individual behaviour. For example, people are often motivated by some of the following:

- high workload and tight deadlines (**pressure**);
- responsibility and authority (**power**);
- exceeding personal goals and targets (**achievement**);
- working as part of a close-knit team (**affiliation**);
- competing against other people (**competition**);
- self-development and personal learning (**growth**);
- praise and recognition from other people (**recognition**);
- earning a good salary (**reward**);
- having a stable and dependable job (**security**);
- working in a well-organized business (**structure**);
- working for a well-respected organization (**prestige**);
- being able to maintain high personal values (**ethics**);
- having a good position (**status**);
- being able to move up an organization (**progression**);
- having control over work activities (**autonomy**);
- the desire to succeed (**achievement**);
- the work ethic, or work itself (**drive**);
- creative and varied work activities (**interest**).

You may have noticed that some of these motivational factors are the same as the values mentioned previously. This goes to show that it is actually quite difficult to untangle values from motivation, and that in all probability they interact with each other. So, if you're the sort of person who places great value on independence you may well be motivated by having control over what you do (**autonomy**), and being able to develop your personal competence and extend your repertoire of skills (**growth**).

Employers find that motivation questionnaires are a good way of comparing job applicants or current employees against job demands; and also against the management style of an organization. The latter is of increasing importance as many businesses are starting to pay attention to their organizational 'culture'. For example, if you have a strong need for structure, clear paths of progression, and security, you might find it difficult to work for a small organisatzon with little in the way of hierarchy or long-term promotion prospects.

An example of a motivation questionnaire is *Motive-A*, published by the Test Agency. Another popular questionnaire is the *Motivation Questionnaire (MQ)* distributed by Saville & Holdsworth Ltd.

Integrity

Integrity is the weasel word used by psychologists when they are talking about honesty; and so integrity tests are designed to discover if you are likely to be an honest and reliable employee. At present, most of these come from the USA and are the result of the adverse publicity generated by polygraph tests. If you are unfamiliar with the polygraph approach it is a lie detector test, which is based on the fact that the electrical resistance of your skin varies when you are telling a lie. This is measured by placing a series of electrical pads on your fingers or hands. It is clearly a rather worrying way of assessing honesty, and also a method that is unacceptable in a selection context.

In consequence, modern integrity tests are questionnaire based and are designed to indicate those aspects of a person's potential work behaviour that may give cause for concern. In many integrity tests the questions relate to how you would respond to a variety of common situations involving money, 'time-theft' and tardiness; and your attitude towards rule breaking and criminality in others. Here are some examples:

- If you found £50 in the street would you hand it in at a police station?
- Would you take a day off 'ill' if you felt you had been over-worked?
- If you received too much change in a shop would you give it back?
- Do you know anybody who steals regularly?

These are fairly obvious questions, but even so they can be quite instructive in showing someone's potential (dis)honesty. Interestingly, there are differences between the sexes in the way that they reply, and also between different countries. Thus, recent research by a major firm of UK test publishers has shown that women are far more likely to return excess change in a shop and that, culturally, of all the European nations, the Spanish are the least likely to give money back. Needless to say these sorts of variations have to be taken into account when applying integrity tests.

Integrity tests are used by retail organizations and other businesses that rely on personal honesty, eg the police, security services, financial organizations and airlines. An example of an integrity test is *Giotto* published by the Psychological Corporation.

Interests

Interest questionnaires are constructed so that they indicate your workplace preferences, or those activities that you feel you would enjoy. Thus, the two main types of interest questionnaires that you will encounter are those assessing management interests; and the more general variety, which measure general occupational interests.

Management interest questionnaires focus on the balance of management functions that are of interest. For example, you will find yourself indicating your level of interest in areas of management such as:

- production and manufacturing;
- technical support and services;
- research and development;
- transport and distribution;
- sales and marketing;
- personnel and training;
- finance and accounts;
- administration and control;
- legal and management services;
- IT and computer systems.

In addition, some questionnaires compare your interest in, say, producing accounts and managing the finances of a business, with the amount of experience you have of doing such a job. This allows an employer to compare your interest, or enthusiasm for something, with your actual experience.

Management questionnaires can also measure your interest in distinct work activities, especially those relating to the day-to-day control of a business. For example:

- written communication;
- oral communication;
- decision making;
- problem solving;
- developing and training;
- negotiating and persuading;
- predicting and forecasting;
- information collection and analysis;
- organizing people and resources.

Such questionnaires are routinely used to assess existing or future managers. However, as with measures of values, they are usually used alongside other sources of information such as personality questionnaires and ability tests.

An example of a management interest questionnaire is the *Management Interest Inventory (MII)*, published by Saville & Holdsworth Ltd.

General occupational interest questionnaires are often used with school leavers, graduates and others to assess interests over the entire range of work activities. One of the best-known systems is that produced by the American psychologist, John Holland, who developed a way of breaking down people's work interests into six main types: Realistic, Investigative, Artistic, Social, Enterprising and Conventional.

- **Realistic** people prefer activities in which they can use practical ways of solving problems. They value concrete things and prefer tangible rewards for their endeavours such as money or status. Realistic people can be described as being genuine, hard-headed, practical and persistent.
- **Investigative** people prefer activities involving a systematic and analytic way of working. They also like tasks involving an observational and scientific approach. Investigative people can be described as being critical, rational, intellectual and curious.
- **Artistic** people place value on individual expression and enjoy language, art, music, drama and writing-based activities. They can be described as being aesthetic, cultural, emotional, intuitive and imaginative.
- **Social** people prefer activities that allow them to influence other people, and to be involved in helping, caring, managing, training, developing and informing. The emphasis is on interpersonal skills, and so social people can be described as being persuasive, understanding, empathic and co-operative.
- **Enterprising** people are concerned with making things happen, and the manipulation of other people and resources to achieve personal success. They often perceive themselves as being aggressive and as possessing leadership abilities. The enterprising person can also be described as being ambitious, energetic, self-confident and adventurous.

● Conventional people prefer activities that involve the detailed and systematic use of information. They like to organize and use data in a precise and disciplined way. They can be described as being conforming, conscientious, methodical and thrifty.

Naturally, it is possible to be a mixture of the above types and to have more than one area of interest. Indeed, this is true of most people, although some combinations are less likely than others, eg conventional and artistic do not often go together, whereas enterprising and social do.

When this system is used in careers guidance the questionnaire yields a three-letter code that indicates your area of interest, eg SEI. This is then used to check against a dictionary of occupational codes containing well over 12,000 different jobs – from abrasive grinder and hassock maker, to uptwister tender and yeast washer. By the way, in the example given, SEI is the code for an occupational psychologist.

An example of an interests questionnaire based on the work of John Holland is the *Self-Directed Search* (*SDS*), which is published by Psychological Assessment Resources Inc in the USA. Other interest questionnaires include *Passport* and the *Rothwell-Miller Interest Blank*, both distributed by The Morrisby Organization, and the *General* and *Advanced Occupational Interest Inventories* (*GOII; AOII*), published by Saville & Holdsworth Ltd.

Finally...

In this chapter the intention has been to introduce you to the idea of personality and the various ways in which it can be measured. Some of you may believe that reducing personality to four or five dimensions is a gross oversimplification. However, before coming to such a conclusion consider the following analogy used in the marketing of a leading US personality questionnaire:

... there are only three primary colours and yet they allow us to produce every single colour, tone and hue in the world...

In a similar way the 'Big Five' personality dimensions allow us to describe the complete spectrum of personality, because when each dimension is broken down into its component scales there are literally millions of different combinations.

Key points

- There are about 1,200 different personality and other self-report questionnaires available to psychologists and employers.
- Type questionnaires place you in a fixed personality category, and are used for development and training purposes.
- Trait questionnaires measure how much of a personality factor you possess. They are used for selection and assessment as they allow you to be directly compared with other people.
- Research has indicated that there are five main dimensions of personality. These cover action, thinking, feeling, relating and conforming.
- There are six main types of questions in personality questionnaires. These include those that force your choice, and those that allow you to rate or rank a series of statements.
- There are a range of strategies that will help you complete any personality questionnaire. These involve being honest (and not second guessing the questionnaire designer); placing your answers in the appropriate context; trusting your first impressions; reading the questions properly; and knowing yourself and the job for which you are applying.
- Some questionnaires contain scales to detect whether you are bending the truth. While there is nothing wrong with presenting yourself in the most positive way, it is very difficult to disguise your real self. The best advice is just to be as honest and straightforward as you can.

- There are many other types of questionnaires apart from those that directly measure personality. For example, questionnaires that assess personal values, integrity, motivation and interests are also common.
- In order to present a strong and consistent picture of your personality you must be positive, open-minded and truthful in your answers. Remember that personality questionnaires are designed to help you find the right job; getting a position on the grounds of inaccurate results is only likely to lead to low performance, and ultimately a great deal of stress.

Top 50 practice test websites

Practice test websites

If you type the phrase 'psychometric test' or 'psychological test' into an internet search engine it will return the addresses of thousands of websites. Unfortunately many of those that claim to provide genuine tests and questionnaires are of extremely low quality. However there are a good number that provide useful practice material if you know where to look!

The websites listed in this section provide thousands of high quality test practice questions, quite apart from a variety of insightful questionnaires. In addition much of this material is available at no cost, or for a small fee.

Top 50 practice websites
General

There are three websites that provide useful background information on psychometric testing, and what the test-taker can expect to happen in the job application and recruitment process.

- **British Psychological Society Testing Centre** (official BPS site): http://www.psychtesting.org.uk.
- **Business Test Publishers Association** (generic UK publishers site): http://www.btpa.org.
- **Chartered Institute of Personnel and Development** (useful articles): http://www.cipd.co.uk.

Ability tests

Many websites cover ability tests, for example:

- **Profiling for Success** (unique ability test linked to this book):
  http://wwwprofilingforsuccess.com/kogan-page.
- **3 Smart Cubes** (range of different tests):
  http://www.3smartcubes.com.
- **Aptitude Hack** (numerical tests):
  http://www.aptitudehack.com.
- **Aviac** (ability tests for pilot selection):
  http://www.aviac.com.
- **Cubiks** (graduate level tests):
  http://practicetests.cubiks.com.
- **Efinancial** (numerical test):
  http://www.efinancialcareers.co.uk.
- **EPSO** (EU civil service 'competition' tests):
  http://europa.eu/epso.
- **Morrisby Organization** (set of six basic aptitude tests):
  http://www.morrisby.com.
- **Practice tests** (range of tests):
  http://www.practicetests.co.uk.
- **PSL/Kenexa** (graduate level tests):
  http://www.psl.co.uk/practice.
- **Psychometric Success** (range of different tests):
  http://www.psychometric-success.com.

- **Qantas Pilot tests** (ability tests used to select pilots – pdf format):
  http://www.qantas.com.au/infodetail/about/employment/qtests.pdf.
- **Saville Consulting** (set of six new practice tests – pdf format):
  http://www.savilleconsulting.com/products.
- **Saville & Holdsworth Ltd** (official SHL practice test site):
  http://www.shldirect.com.
- **University of Kent Careers Service** (range of tests):
  http://www.kent.ac.uk/careers/psychotests.htm.

IQ tests

If you want to complete a test that will give you an idea of your IQ, then try one or more of the following:

- **Mensa** (Mensa 'workout'):
  http://www.mensa.org.
- **High IQ Society** (IQ tests & puzzles):
  http://www.highiqsociety.org.
- **GIQ test** (full length IQ test):
  http://www.giqtest.com.

Personality questionnaires

There are plenty of websites that host personality and similar questionnaires. Here's a selection of some of the best:

- **Adaptiv** (resilience questionnaire):
  http://www.adaptivlearning.com.
- **BBC Science** (range of questionnaires):
  http://www.bbc.co.uk/science/humanbody/mind/index_surveys.shtml.

- **Keirsey Type Indicator** (psychological type indicator): http://www.keirsey.com.
- **NEO Personality test** (psychological trait questionnaire): http://www.personalitytest.net/ipip/ipipneol.htm.
- **People Profiler** (work attributes questionnaire): http://www.peopleprofiler.co.uk.
- **Personality Project** (psychological trait questionnaire): http://test.personality-project.org.
- **Psychology Today** (range of questionnaires): http://www.psychologytoday.com/pto/self-tests.php.
- **Team Technology** (psychological type indicator): http://www.teamtechnology.co.uk/mmdi-re/mmdi-re.htm.

Leadership style questionnaires

Leadership style questionnaires are often used in staff development programmes. Two questionnaires that will help you explore your style are:

- **DTI Inspired Leadership** (government sponsored questionnaire): http://www.inspiredleadership.org.uk.
- **Formula 4 Leadership** (based on four key leadership types): http://www.formula4leadership.com/menu_questions.htm.

Learning style questionnaires

An appreciation of your learning style is valuable if you are considering further education or training. Find out about your style using these questionnaires:

- **VARK** (based on four factor model of learning styles): http://www.vark-learn.com.
- **Memletics** (based on seven factor model of learning styles): http://www.learning-styles-online.com.

Careers interest and career planning questionnaires

There are some really good careers interest and careers planning resources available, especially for younger people. Try some of these:

- Career Key (based on Holland model):
  http://www.careerkey.org.
- Career Zone (based on Holland model):
  http://www.nycareerzone.org.
- Oscar (career interest and values questionnaire):
  http://www.ioscar.org/tx/oscar.asp.
- Windmills (complete career planning tool):
  http://www.windmillsonline.co.uk/interactive.

UK University admissions tests

For those who have to take a university admissions test there are a variety of useful practice resources. Some of these, such as Dr Test, also link to material that is valuable in preparing for graduate and managerial job applications.

- Dr Test (best site for all admissions tests):
  http://www.drtest.co.uk.
- BioMedical Admissions Test (BMAT):
  http://www.bmat.org.uk.
- Graduate Medical School Admissions Test (GAMSAT):
  http://www.gamsat.co.uk.
- History Aptitude Test (HAT):
  http://www.history.ox.ac.uk.
- Law School Admission Council (LNAT practice):
  http://www.lsac.org.
- Modern and Medieval Languages test (MML):
  http://www.mml.cam.ac.uk.

- **National Admissions Test for Law** (LNAT):
  http://www.lnat.ac.uk.
- **Physics Aptitude Test:**
  http://www.physics.ox.ac.uk.
- **Sixth Term Examination Papers** (STEP):
  http://www.maths.cam.ac.uk.
- **Training & Development Agency for Schools** (QTS tests):
  http://www.tda.gov.uk/skillstests.aspx.
- **Thinking Skills Assessment** (TSA):
  http://www.tsa.ucles.org.uk.
- **UK Clinical Aptitude test** (UKCAT):
  http://www.ukcat.ac.uk.
- **University College London** (BMAT practice):
  http://www.ucl.ac.uk/lapt/bmat.

Note: This list is based on a regularly updated web page that can be found at
www.markparkinson.co.uk/psychometric_links.htm.

Appendix

Competencies

The word 'competency' is widely used in business and personnel psychology, and refers to the behaviours that are necessary to achieve the objectives of an organization. A competency is also something you can measure; and lists of competencies form a common language for describing how people perform in different situations.

Every job can be described in terms of key competencies. This means that they can be used for all forms of assessment, including appraisals, training needs analysis and selection. In fact, it is in the selection context, especially in advertizements, that you are most likely to come across competencies. For example, the following were recently used in a recruitment campaign for a major UK car retailer:

> You will have good **interpersonal** and **communication skills**, and have substantial personal **impact**. Also familiar with IT systems, you will enjoy **problem solving**, and make the best use of your **analytic skills** ... This is a job that requires an **innovative** approach, coupled with a commitment to **teamwork**. You will be **quality focused**, and committed to building on our enviable reputation in the industry.

This is quite a typical list containing eight different competencies. It is these sorts of competencies that personnel professionals aim to detect by examining your application details, and through assessment processes such as psychometric testing and interviewing.

Different competencies

The competencies that follow are all commonly used in job specifications, and form the criteria against which to assess people. I have described each one and indicated if it can be assessed using a psychometric test or questionnaire. You can use this list, in conjunction with job advertizements, to decide which aspects of your ability or personality may be assessed by the tests you are asked to complete. Surveys have shown that the most popular competencies asked for are communication, leadership, judgement, initiative, motivation, analytic skills, planning, innovation, interpersonal skills and numeracy.

Individual competencies – your personal attributes

- **Flexibility** – This is the ability to change direction, or modify the way in which you do something. It includes a willingness to try, adaptability and a positive outlook.
  Measurement: Personality or Motivation Questionnaire.
- **Decisiveness** – This is a readiness to act and to take decisions. It involves making a balanced judgement and taking the appropriate actions.
  Measurement: Personality Questionnaire.
- **Tenacity** – This is the ability to persevere and stick with a problem until it is solved. It is also marked by the ability to abandon a problem if it is unsolvable.
  Measurement: Personality Questionnaire.
- **Independence** – This is a willingness to question the accepted way of doing things; also the strength of mind to pursue a course of action based on your own convictions.
  Measurement: Personality or Values Questionnaire.

- **Risk Taking** – The extent to which you are prepared to take calculated risks. An important factor in many jobs including sales and manufacturing.
  Measurement: Personality or Values Questionnaire.
- **Personal Integrity** – The maintenance of high personal standards; also the implementation of appropriate ethical and moral norms in a work context.
  Measurement: Personality, Integrity or Values Questionnaire.

Interpersonal competencies – dealing with other people

- **Communication** – The ability to convey information clearly and accurately, both orally and in writing; also includes a recognition of the importance of actively listening to others.
  Measurement: Verbal Reasoning Test (for written communication).
- **Impact** – The skill of creating an immediate and positive first impression on other people. A vital ability for many managerial and selling positions.
  Measurement: Personality Questionnaire.
- **Persuasiveness** – The ability to persuade and influence others to your point of view. This also involves being seen as believable and authoritative.
  Measurement: Personality Questionnaire or Specialist Sales Personality Questionnaire (if appropriate).
- **Personal Awareness** – This is being aware of other people and the environment in which they operate. It means taking into account other people's thoughts and feelings before acting.
  Measurement: Personality Questionnaire.
- **Teamwork** – This means contributing in an active and co-operative way with other team members. It includes supporting other people, and making decisions by consensus.

- *Measurement: Personality Questionnaire or Team Role Indicator.*
- **Openness** – This is being able to encourage different points of view without becoming defensive; also the ability to build on the contributions from other people.
  Measurement: Personality Questionnaire.

Analytical competencies – the elements of decision making

- **Innovation** – The ability to come up with imaginative and practical solutions to business problems.
  Measurement: Personality or Creativity Questionnaire or specialist Ability Test.
- **Analytic Skills** – The ability to break a situation down into its component parts, recognize what needs to be done and plan a suitable course of action in a step-by-step way.
  Measurement: Critical Reasoning Test.
- **Numerical Problem Solving** – The ability to understand and analyse numerical information. This includes financial data and statistics presented in reports, tables, graphs, charts, etc.
  Measurement: Numerical Reasoning Test.
- **Problem Solving** – The ability to evaluate a situation and to identify an appropriate solution that meets the customers' needs – the skill of 'turning a problem into a solution'.
  Measurement: Critical Reasoning Test.
- **Practical Learning** – This involves being able to absorb and learn new methods, and then applying them to job-related activities.
  Measurement: Specialist Ability Test or Learning Styles Questionnaire.
- **Detail Consciousness** – The ability to process large amounts of complex information. This includes all forms of written, verbal and visual data.
  Measurement: Ability Test or Personality Questionnaire.

Managerial competencies – taking charge of other people

- **Leadership** – This is being able to take the role of a leader and guiding the actions of other people accordingly. The focus is on achieving results by working through other people.
  Measurement: Personality Questionnaire or Leadership Style Questionnaire.

- **Empowerment** – This is the concern for developing other people, and giving them the authority and responsibility to act on their own volition.
  Measurement: Specialist Personality Questionnaire or Values Questionnaire.

- **Strategic Planning** – This is the ability to maintain a broad overview ('helicopter' view) of business activities, which allows you to plan for the future.
  Measurement: Personality Questionnaire or specialist Ability Test.

- **Corporate Sensitivity** – This is the demonstration of an understanding of where a business is going, and of its agreed goals and strategies.
  Measurement: Personality or Interests Questionnaire.

- **Project Management** – The ability to define the requirements of a project and to lead a group of people towards a specified goal.
  Measurement: Specialist Personality Questionnaire or Team Role Indicator.

- **Management Control** – The appreciation that businesses need to be controlled and that the work of subordinates needs to be organized.
  Measurement: Specialist Personality Questionnaire or Management Interests Indicator.

Motivational competencies – the things that drive you

- **Resilience** – The ability to 'bounce back' in the face of adversity or when things do not go according to plan.
  Measurement: Personality Questionnaire.
- **Energy** – The personal store of energy that you bring to work, which helps you maintain a high level of performance – your 'stamina' or 'drive'.
  Measurement: Personality Questionnaire or Motivation Questionnaire.
- **Motivation** – This is the ability to motivate yourself *and* those around you. It's also related to knowing when to take control of a situation, and when to issue orders to other people.
  Measurement: Personality or Motivation Questionnaire.
- **Achievement Orientation** – This is the drive to achieve results, and to set targets that provide personal challenges.
  Measurement: Personality, Values or Motivation Questionnaire.
- **Initiative** – This is the ability to work in a proactive way to anticipate events, and to act on opportunities as they arise.
  Measurement: Personality Questionnaire.
- **Quality Focus** – This is the commitment to getting a job done well, and to recognizing that the quality of a product or service is of critical importance.
  Measurement: Specialist Personality or Values Questionnaire.

The preceding list is by no means exhaustive but it should give you an idea of the sort of competencies required by employers. You should also recognize that some of these competencies are difficult to measure with psychometric tests alone (especially those that I have indicated as needing 'specialist' measures), and many are assessed using a combination of methods, eg tests, interviews and group exercises involving a number of candidates.

Group exercises

Group exercises are designed to assess your problem-solving abilities, and responses to other people, in typical work situations. In some ways they are similar to the business learning exercises described in Chapter 3, but they involve a combination of both interpersonal and analytical skills. The following example will give you an idea of what is involved.

The runway exercise

'You are a member of a group of four planning officers who have to decide on the location of a new runway for a major regional airport. You have at your disposal a range of maps, plans, costings, economic surveys and the results of a local planning inquiry.

'The task is to decide which one of three options best balances the demands of the regional economy, the local population and the environment. The group has two-and-a-half hours to produce an argued recommendation.'

This sort of exercise typically produces a range of arguments both for and against all the options. For example, in this case some of the key issues include the following:

Option 1:   Easy access to motorway and rail systems
Strong support from regional businesses
Enthusiastic backing from local Member of Parliament
but ...
Most expensive (£2.5 million)
Will destroy habitat of rare bird species
Requires some compulsory land purchase
Option 2:   Least expensive (£1.8 million)
Uses some existing derelict land
Preserves habitat of rare birds
but ...

May produce a slight noise problem
Location makes it most difficult to build
Opposition from local pressure groups

Option 3: Costs £2 million (£3 million minus £1 million grant aid)
Requires no compulsory land purchase
Has room for business park (creating 2,500 new jobs)
but ...
Is opposed by national conservation groups
Requires a 'greenfield' site
May create a long-term pollution problem.

Which option would you choose?

If you are ever faced with one of these exercises, the most important thing to remember is that there isn't one perfect solution. What the assessors are looking for are reasoned and logical arguments, which take into account all the information provided. It's also important that all members of the group agree on the solution, and consequently that decisions are made on a consensual basis. Should you require any further information on group exercises the best place to look is in books that include chapters on Assessment Centres, eg *Your Job Search Made Easy*, published by Kogan Page.

Answers: SHL® practice tests (technical, clerical and graduate)

Series 1

Test 1: Working with Words 1 = A, 2 = B, 3 = E, 4 = C, 5 = E, 6 = D.

Test 2: Working with Numbers 1 = D, 2 = C, 3 = D, 4 = E, 5 = B, 6 = C, 7 = B, 8 = A.

Test 3: Working with Diagrams 1 = A, 2 = E, 3 = C, 4 = A, 5 = B, 6 = D.

Test 4: Checking Information 1 = A, 2 = E, 3 = B, D, 4 = A, B, D, 5 = E, 6 = A, B, C, 7 = B, D, 8 = B, C, 9 = E, 10 = A, B, C, D.

Test 5: Recognizing Shapes 1 = A, 2 = C, 3 = B, 4 = D, 5 = C, 6 = B.

Test 6: Mechanical Understanding 1 = A, 2 = C, 3 = B, 4 = B.

Series 2

Test 1: Interpreting Written Information 1 = A, 2 = B, 3 = C, 4 = A, 5 = C, 6 = B, 7 = B, 8 = A.

Test 2: Interpreting Data 1 = D, 2 = A, 3 = B, 4 = C, 5 = E, 6 = C.

Test 3: Interpreting Diagrams: 1 = C, 2 = E, 3 = B, 4 = A, 5 = D, 6 = E.

Series 3

Test 1: Verbal Reasoning 1 = B, 2 = A, 3 = B, 4 = C, 5 = C, 6 = B, 7 = A, 8 = C.

Test 2: Numerical Reasoning 1 = A, 2 = B, 3 = C, 4 = B, 5 = E, 6 = D.

Test 3: Diagrammatic Reasoning 1 = C, 2 = B, 3 = E, 4 = B, 5 = D, 6 = A.

Answers: TFL graduate tests and thinking skills assessment

Test 1: Abstract reasoning. Question 1 = (a) B, (b) A, (c) Neither, (d) A, (e) B, (f) B; Question 2 = (a) B, (b) Neither, (c) A, (d) A, (e) A, (f) Neither; Question 3 = (a) Neither, (b) A, (c) A, (d) B, (e) Neither, (f) A.

Test 2: Verbal reasoning. Question 1 = (a) F, (b) T, (c) F, (d) F, (e) CT; Question 2 = (a) T, (b) CT, (c) T, (d) CT, (e) F; Question 3 = (a) F, (b) CT, (c) T, (d) CT, (e) T.

Test 3: Numerical reasoning. Question 1 = (a) e, (b) b, (c) a, (d) b, (e) c; Question 2 = (a) e, (b) d, (c) c, (d) b, (e) c; Question 3 = (a) c, (b) c, (c) a, (d) d, (e) e.

Thinking Skills Assessment:
Question 1 = (d); Question 2 = (a); Question 3 = (c); Question 4 = (a); Question 5 = (b); Question 6 = (b).

Further reading from Kogan Page

Interview and Career Guidance

The A–Z of Careers and Jobs, 15th edition, Susan Hodgson, 2008

Careers and Jobs in IT, David Yardley, 2004

Careers and Jobs in the Media, Simon Kent, 2005

Careers and Jobs in Nursing, Linda Nazarko, 2004

Careers and Jobs in Travel and Tourism, Verité Reily Collins, 2004

Choosing Your Career, 2nd edition, Sally Longson, 2004

Great Answers to Tough Interview Questions, 7th edition, Martin Yate, 2008

Odd Jobs, 2nd edition, Simon Kent, 2002

Online Job Hunting, Martin Yate and Terra Dourlain, 2002

Preparing the Perfect CV, 6th edition, Rebecca Corfield, 2006

Preparing the Perfect Job Application, 4th edition, Rebecca Corfield, 2007

Readymade CVs, 3rd edition, Lynn Williams, 2004

Readymade Job Search Letters, 3rd edition, Lynn Williams, 2004

The Ultimate CV Book, Martin Yate, 2002

The Ultimate Interview Book, Lynn Williams, 2005

The Ultimate Job Search Letters Book, Martin Yate, 2003
Your Job Search Made Easy, 3rd edition, Mark Parkinson, 2002

Titles in the Testing Series

Aptitude, Personality and Motivation Tests: Assess Your Potential and Plan Your Career, 2nd edition, Jim Barrett, 2004

The Aptitude Test Workbook, Jim Barrett, 2003

Career, Aptitude and Selection Tests, 2nd edition, Jim Barrett, 2006

Great Answers to Tough Interview Questions: How to Get the Job You Want, 6th edition, Martin John Yate, 2005

How to Master Personality Questionnaires, 2nd edition, Mark Parkinson, 2000

How to Pass Advanced Aptitude Tests, Jim Barrett, 2008

How to Pass Advanced Numeracy Tests, Mike Byron, 2008

How to Pass the Civil Service Qualifying Tests, 2nd edition, Mike Bryon, 2003

How to Pass Computer Selection Tests, Sanjay Modha, 1994

How to Pass Graduate Psychometric Tests, 3rd edition, Mike Bryon, 2001

How to Pass the New Police Selection System, revised 2nd edition, Harry Tolley, Billy Hodge and Catherine Tolley, 2007

How to Pass Numeracy Tests, 3rd edition, Harry Tolley and Ken Thomas, 2006

How to Pass Numerical Reasoning Tests, Heidi Smith, 2006

How to Pass the Police Initial Recruitment Test, Ken Thomas, Catherine Tolley and Harry Tolley, 2004

How to Pass Professional Level Psychometric Tests, 2nd edition, Sam Al-Jajjoka, 2004

How to Pass Selection Tests, 3rd edition, Mike Bryon and Sanjay Modha, 2005

How to Pass Technical Selection Tests, Mike Bryon, 2005

How to Pass Verbal Reasoning Tests, 3rd edition, Harry Tolley and Ken Thomas, 2006

How to Succeed at an Assessment Centre, 2nd edition, Harry Tolley and Robert Wood, 2005

IQ and Psychometric Tests, 2nd edition, Philip Carter, 2007

Preparing the Perfect CV: How to Improve Your Chances of Getting the Job You Want, 4th edition, Rebecca Corfield, 2006

Preparing the Perfect Job Application, 4th edition, Rebecca Corfield, 2007

Readymade CVs: Sample CVs for Every Type of Job, 3rd edition, Lynn Williams, 2004

Readymade Job Search Letters: Every Type of Letter for Getting the Job You Want, 3rd edition, Lynn Williams, 2004

Successful Interview Skills, Rebecca Corfield, 4th edition, 2006

Test Your Numerical Aptitude, Jim Barrett, 2007

The Numeracy Test Workbook, Mike Bryon, 2006

CD ROMS

Psychometric Tests, Volume 1, *The Times* Testing Series, Editor Mike Bryon 2002

Test Your Aptitude, Volume 1, *The Times* Testing Series, Editor Mike Bryon, 2002

Test Your IQ, Volume 1, *The Times* Testing Series, Editor Mike Bryon, 2002